new**Brazilian**gardens

roberto silva

new
Brazilian
gardens

the legacy of Burle Marx

with 278 illustrations,
268 in color

Thames & Hudson

To Irene Ferreira da Silva

Half-title *Heliconia rostrata*.
Title Piracaia Garden.
Contents (top to bottom) Alex Hanazaki,
residencia in Guarujá; Alex Hanazaki, residencia in
São Paulo; Orlando Busarello, Urban Oasis; Orlando
Busarello, Urban Oasis.

First published in 2006 in hardcover in the
United States of America by Thames & Hudson Inc.,
500 Fifth Avenue, New York, New York 10110

thamesandhudsonusa.com

Library of Congress Catalog Card Number
2005906276

ISBN-13: 978-0-500-51286-9
ISBN-10: 0-500-51286-8

Printed in China by Midas Printing Ltd

contents

introduction 6

introduction

The flora of the new world was so exotic to the Europeans' eyes that
many explorers truly believed they had arrived at the true Garden of Eden.

William Howard Adams

In the 1930s and 1940s a group of talented and daring designers began to transform the landscapes of the world. In America, Garrett Eckbo liberated the formal axis of the traditional Beaux-Arts style with his asymmetrical and curvilinear gardens. Thomas Church, best known for his work at the Donnell garden, Sonoma, and influenced by Art Deco and Cubism, created organic and zigzag shapes, with vegetation used as a structural material. Mexican designer Luis Barragán dazzled and surprised with his use of colour, monolithic walls and water channels. And, conceiving gardens as abstract paintings and making skilful use of his native Brazilian flora, Roberto Burle Marx dominated the landscape-design profession for almost half of the twentieth century.

From the mid- to late twentieth century these designers and their followers played a critical role in shaping our landscapes and environments. In an endless cycle of innovation and creativity, designers from around the world, such as Americans Kathryn Gustafson and Martha Schwartz, the Spaniard Fernando Caruncho and Dan Pearson in Britain, have shown an increased awareness of environmental issues, combined with an understanding of both past developments and contemporary practices. They have reclaimed, cross-fertilized and translated elements of modern art in our outdoor spaces, transforming dull voids left by architects into remarkable places to live. As a result, their work has been covered extensively in the international media.

But what is happening now in Brazil? What legacy has the great Burle Marx left in his native country? And what can we learn from today's landscape designers in a country so rich in natural resources, and which enjoys a generous climate that allows tropical plants from all over the world to be transplanted, grow and flourish?

INFLUENCES

To answer these questions and understand how Brazilian landscapes and gardens have evolved into what they are today it is important to know some history. From the arrival of the Portuguese in Brazil in 1500, and throughout the Colonial period, the image of the country was dominated by its dramatic natural scenery and untamed vegetation. It was only in the seventeenth century that the first attempts were made to control this natural wilderness and create man-made landscapes. Largely urban in character, early examples can be seen in Recife and Olinda, and later, at the end of the eighteenth century, in Rio de Janeiro. The Passeio Publico in Rio de Janeiro, designed by Mestre Valentim in 1783, is perhaps the most important project of this period.

In the nineteenth century the reign of Dom Pedro II witnessed a major period of reform, encompassing cultural and social transformations, population increase and changing customs and habits. Pedro II called for engineers and scientists, French artists and botanists to ensure that Brazil kept up to date with the fashions and scientific progress of Europe. It was during this cultural efflorescence that Rio de Janeiro's botanical gardens were created, the first studies of nature were made and the architect Grandjean de Montigny introduced classical-style architecture. Plants were imported from abroad, acclimatized and displayed in borders in parks and gardens – most of them reflecting the latest French and English styles.

Auguste François de Glaziou was a significant landscape architect in Rio de Janeiro in this period. Arriving in Brazil from France in 1858, he worked first as a hydraulic engineer but then developed an interest in Brazilian flora. He was later invited to work for the department of parks and gardens and created numerous court palaces, including

Quinta da Boa Vista and São Cristóvão, as well as public spaces such as Praça da República and Campo da Santana; he was also responsible for the restoration of the Passeio Publico in Rio de Janeiro. Glaziou's main contribution to the Brazilian landscape was his combination of traditional French formality in the design of his layouts with the use of exuberant Brazilian flora.

Alongside these grand gardens, whether in public spaces or aristocratic houses, examples of minor landscapes began to appear in agricultural areas away from the cities. Ornamental plants were used to enhance the beauty of fazendas and houses even in small villages, and they also began to appear around churches and monasteries.

In this modernist garden designed by Haruyoshi Ono for Burle Marx & Cia, the influence of Burle Marx is evident in the strong lines and varied textures. Water cascades down the uneven surface of the wall into the reflecting pool, harmonizing effortlessly with the architecture – the work of Chico Goveia. Planting includes massed groundcover, such as *Dietes iridioides*, while the aquatic *Cyperus papyrus* and heliconias add dramatic effects to this otherwise apparently simple scheme.

From this period right up until the 1920s, Brazil's major cultural influences continued to come from Europe. Aristocratic families were given European-style educations and emulated European manners and fashions. In order to be considered civilized and to achieve status in high society in cities such as Rio de Janeiro and São Paulo, the élite imported objects, customs and ideas from Europe – anything that originated in Brazil was considered to be in poor taste and of low quality.

A wave of immigrants from Italy, Portugal and Germany around this time brought new construction materials, techniques and styles – one notable development being Art Nouveau, known as the 'Floral Style' in Brazil. In addition, the European immigrants also helped to introduce gardening as a hobby, as well as the practice of displaying and arranging flowers inside the house.

It was not until the early phase of modernism (1922–30) that intellectuals, writers and artists started a cultural revolution that questioned such contemporary Brazilian values. These thinkers rejected anything European or American in search of true Brazilian culture, including acknowledging its indigenous populations, such as the Tupi-Guarani. Oswald de Andrade, a writer and leader of the movement, published *Revista de Antropofagia*, which features cannibalism as a concept; he presented the Brazilian people with the challenge, 'Tupi or not tupi, that is the question'. The message spread through the country as a 'literature that authoritatively located its own originality in a kind of anthropological and cultural crossbreeding that took no account of racism and colonialism in its ritual and cannibalistic digestion of European culture'. Other artists joined the movement, including the writer Mario de Andrade and painters Tarsila do Amaral and Candido Portinari.

THE IMPACT OF ROBERTO BURLE MARX

It was in the context of this new-found appreciation of native culture in the early 1930s that Roberto Burle Marx began to create gardens that incorporated primary colours, organic shapes, indigenous graphic design and Cubism. On his return from a period staying in Germany – where he had first discovered and painted Brazilian flora in the Berlin botanical garden – Burle Marx found himself with a mission to create a new language of landscape design in Brazil. His approach was completely individual, with no connection to, or derivation from, previous modernist movements, and it was also utterly unlike either

Europe's Art Nouveau or the American modernists such as Eckbo, Church and Lawrence Halprin. Through his training as an artist, together with his associations with major architects and urbanites such as Lucio Costa, Rino Levi and Oscar Niemeyer, his passion for native Brazilian plants and his sheer creative genius, Burle Marx became one of the most significant landscape architects of the twentieth century.

During his lifetime he designed over 3,000 projects in Brazil and around the world. Among his most celebrated works are the Copacabana Promenade, the Odette Monteiro Residence, the Ministry of Education and Health building in Rio de Janeiro and the public gardens and palaces in the capital Brasília. Still today, his distinctive style inspires designers working both in Brazil and internationally, in projects that mix expanses of grasses with perennials and designs where abstraction, the sweeping colour of a single species and texture combine to create a dynamic unity.

Brazil continues to celebrate his designs, not only in landscapes but in many different media, including jewelry, fashion and textile design. More than simply a landscape designer, he is a Brazilian trademark – certainly familiar to the thousands of tourists and passers-by who cross the sinuous waves of his Copacabana beach pavement. Burle Marx is a major point of reference for the new generation of gardeners and designers.

CONTEMPORARY BRAZILIAN GARDENS

Over the past twenty years Brazilian landscaping has been changing and developing new strategies to face twenty-first century challenges. Among the issues to be addressed are urban regeneration in the big cities, the relocating of public spaces within them, the preservation of historical landscapes and the conservation of nature reserves, along with the establishment of landscape design courses for the next generation of designers.

Although today there are perhaps fewer large-scale projects, and Brazil continues to experience intermittent economic crises, the new designers can take advantage of working in a country where a combination of inexpensive labour and corporate and private wealth presents them with opportunities to build some exceptional gardens. They are also liberated by the fact that in Brazil the weight of historical layers is not as oppressive as in the Old World, freeing them

up to create a new language of garden design. Small private practices have been able to realize significant projects in residential locations, condominiums, recreational areas, hotels and resorts. This contemporary generation has respected and absorbed the legacy of Burle Marx, while at the same time assimilating developments taking place in America, Europe and Japan.

Show gardens present another opportunity for designers to work on unusual designs, generating innovative ideas. 'Casa Cor' is Brazil's

opposite In these three distinctive projects, Burle Marx demonstrated his skilful use of plant material and hardscaping. On the far left is a Burle Marx trademark: the architectural tree *Beaucarnea recurvata* planted among boulders. In the centre, in an example of Burle Marx's more naturalistic planting style, the yellow *Sedum multiceps* forms a bright spreading carpet in a rocky landscape. On the right, Burle Marx used the stunning Flamboyant tree

(*Delonix regia*) as a backdrop for the spiky bromeliads planted in a massive sculptural wall made from reclaimed architectural stone.
above Haruyoshi Ono created this perfectly unified landscape around a colonial farmhouse, its guesthouse and chapel, set in a wooded landscape. The existing pond was reshaped and large expanses of aquatic plants were introduced. A wooden bridge connects the chapel to the main house.

most important house and garden show, an annual event that moves each month to a different state. In a selected house, an emerging professional designs one of the rooms, whether it is the bathroom, living room, kitchen – or garden space. This showcase provides a valuable platform to promote new talents, including many of those whose work is illustrated in this book.

In Brazil's contemporary landscapes we find a fusion of past and present. Like a continuous act of cannibalism, practitioners have been able to absorb, digest, adapt and translate the diversity of different garden traditions to create something distinctively Brazilian. The influence of European classicism still makes its presence felt in these gardens, as does the American modernist tradition, for instance in the work of Luciano Fiaschi. The abstraction and bold shapes of Burle Marx's designs live on in projects by Jamil Jose Kfouri and others. The

late twentieth century's ecology movement is well represented, while the influence of the contemporary information age can be seen in the theatrical landscapes of avant-garde designers such as Gilberto Elkis and Alex Hanazaki.

LOOKING TO THE NEW GENERATION

While much has been written about Burle Marx, there is no book dedicated to the many other designers who have contributed to modern Brazilian landscape design. Several of these designers have themselves become influences in their own turn, and they continue to create landscapes that are varied and individual. The purpose of this book is to illustrate and describe some of the finest examples of gardens and landscapes designed by Brazil's new generation during the past ten years or so. Selected from all over Brazil – from Rio de

Janeiro, Parana, Pernambuco, Minas Gerais and São Paulo – the projects illustrate the diversity of Brazil's gardens and their special character, but they also incorporate universal ideas that can be translated to any country.

Of the designers featured, some are still relative newcomers, while others, such as Isabel Duprat, Gilberto Elkis and Lucia Porto, are well-established names in garden design. All are a true reflection of a country that, despite its economic instability and sometimes chaotic nature, is able to create outdoor spaces of originality and outstanding beauty.

opposite Two types of grass in different shades of green create a chequerboard motif in this design by Burle Marx; the squares are edged by metal frames. Planting in the orthogonal herbaceous borders consists of large expanses of daylilies (*Hemerocallis* sp.) with dramatic *Phormium tenax* used as accent plants. The modernist three-dimensional concrete mural works as a strong background to the colourful and free planting.

above Hardscaping consisting of Portuguese mosaic in three colours – black, white and red – forms an integral part of Haruyoshi Ono's design for a recreational area in a park. The continuous flowing lines create a sense movement around the central circular water feature, the shape of which is echoed by concentric planting beds and concrete seating.

water

water

The pool is a place to gather around, much as a fireplace is in a room.
It offers swimming for the athlete or just getting wet if you are hot.

Thomas Church

As a natural element, water can bring perhaps more character to a landscape and garden than any single plant or other feature. In fact, all gardens can benefit from the calm it brings. Water always deserves its place, whether as an expansive or a modest-sized pool, or even a simple ornamental pond in the back garden.

It is an element that constantly fascinates and delights. According to its position in the garden, we respond instinctively to its moods, are enriched by its soothing properties or beguiled by its constant movement. Swimming pools can add a feeling of playfulness, as

well as architectural impact to the surroundings. A simple reflecting water feature encourages contemplation, while mirroring everything around it. If there is the space, and the inclination, cascades and fountains can impart elegance and grandeur to a garden or landscape.

Beyond water's visual appeal is the effect its sound can have. Flowing water in a stream represents fluidity and suggests how rough edges can be moulded and smoothed to different shapes over time – reminding us, perhaps, how we should move through and

previous pages Mirror by the Sea (p. 47).

left In response to a request for a garden to accommodate the client's sculpture, Isabel Duprat created this cool and minimal space. The tall white wall highlights the artwork, reflected in the streamlined pool.

opposite above left Private pool as resort: occupying a central place, this large swimming pool by Alex Hanazaki for a garden in Guarujá combines several options. A slope functions as a beach for the children, while a Phoenix palm separates an area for water games; at the deep end dark blue tiles challenge divers. The pool also features a waterfall with a hydro-massage.

opposite above right Well integrated within the landscape and almost immersed in natural vegetation, this elegant pool, designed by Luiz Vieira in the Porto de Galinha area of Recife, is like a small piece of the sea.

adapt to life's experiences. And even if there is no man-made water feature, the mere observation of a water drop on leaves after rain can reflect the mystery that surrounds us.

In Brazil water is everywhere. Travelling by air, one sees a breathtaking coastline of blue sea fringed with coconut trees and exotic flora. In the country and city, rivers criss-cross the Brazilian landscape as a complex and interconnected network of watery veins. Rivers evoke the feeling of opportunity and exploration – the thought that we can travel along them by boat, transporting us from one state to another, or from one city to the next, cheaply and without damage to the environment. Given the hectic pace of modern living, this is perhaps a quaint notion, but it provides an enduring dream for those seeking adventure or romance.

In gardens water reflects and draws in the ever-changing surrounding scenery as a refreshing element during hot, bright and sunny days that seem to last forever in Brazil. It is unimaginable to design or live in a garden here without considering some form of water feature or pool. In the wide range of examples that follow, water is used in a variety of ways as an integral and essential part of the design.

The first section of the chapter focuses on water features used as a particular focus or for spectacular effect, as in the fantastic sculptural space and naturalistic cascades designed by Luiz Vieira for the Atlanta Plaza hotel, located in the famous Boa Viagem beach area of Recife. A water feature does not have to be large to be effective, as designer

Marcelo Faisal demonstrates in a small urban space in São Paulo – and does not even have to contain water.

A circular patio completely surrounded by water and aquatic plants could not be a more perfect place to have breakfast, as seen in the Piracaia garden, where the water flows naturally down the slope from pool to pool as if finding its way to the water beyond. And if you want to immerse yourself completely in the element, you can choose either to walk beneath waterfalls or bathe in a pool heated by a sun-soaked rock as the evening settles on an orientally influenced garden by Barbara Uccello and Maringa Pilz.

The second part of the chapter looks at swimming pools, often both a starting point and culmination of the entire garden design process. The organic lines of a pool designed by Gil Fialho effortlessly seem to echo the forms of the mountains of the surrounding landscape, while the abstraction of the wacky design of Jamil Jose Kfouri's communal pool for a large residential building produces a dazzling visual effect.

In Evani Kuperman Franco's design for the pool of a house on the coast at Guarujá, the ethereal and everlasting blue sea apparently merges with the pool into infinity. Water is here integrated into the landscape at the point where the garden makes the transition between the lawn and the native vegetation of the forest. And in Sergio Menon's design for pool for a residence in Iporanga, the calm, tranquil surface of the water acts a mirror, reflecting the serenity of the beauty around it.

left When the water feature in this garden had to be replaced, Faisal retained its fluid lines using both swathes of single species planting and beige pebbles in a liquid shape. Carefully placed stones and plants such as bamboo and *Acer palmatum* enhance the feeling of natural order. **below** A place for resting in the garden, with seats and tables in the shade of the canopy of the fruit tree *Myrciaria cauliflora*.

01 a secluded garden

marcelo faisal | designer
location | são paulo

Marcelo Faisal is one of those bright young talents that emerge in the Brazilian design profession every year. Having studied first as an agronomist and later as an architect, he has his feet firmly on the ground while his imagination roams freely. 'I always had an interest in the land before becoming a garden designer. The only example I knew was Burle Marx,' he says, 'but as an architect I learned how to value the architecture in the exterior space.'

His landscape style is clearly influenced both by the work of Roberto Burle Marx and by the time Faisal spent in Rio de Janeiro discovering about plants. He increased his knowledge further through experiences in the countryside, in orchards, country gardens and farms. Over time, Faisal has strengthened his lines and developed a language that now has a particular trademark: the use of indigenous plants within a confident, graphic layout. This combination is evident in the exquisite small garden he has created in a residential area of São Paulo – a jewel concealed behind high, grey concrete buildings. Constructed and planted as a patio garden next to a modern house, the space is surrounded by tall, white walls in a setting of severe linearity. Faisal introduced a less rigid layout to break up the lines and used informal planting to soften them.

As the focal point of the project he originally created a water feature, intended to enhance and echo the relaxed layout with its organic shape. Later, for reasons of safety, the water feature had to be replaced. However, Faisal cleverly retained the concept and the liquid form of the original design, using beige pebbles and black grass instead of water, so that the water still flows, but now in the form of a dry river.

Around this feature Faisal used a combination of plants with contrasting textures and shapes. The rounded forms of the pruned *Rhododendron simsii* work well with the spikiness of *Dietes bicolor*, while the tall canes of the bamboo *Phyllostachys pubescens* create verticality around the edges. The vigorous and spreading *Eichhornia crassipes* in the original planting counterpointed the sense of order conveyed by the *Viburnum suspensum*.

To create height and balance, Faisal included tall specimens of *Magnolia x soulangeana* and *Acer palmatum*. In addition to bringing an immediate feeling of maturity to the garden, these also add colour and a sense of progression in different seasons. The acer can be appreciated for its ever-changing leaf hues throughout the year, while the fleeting magnolia blooms introduce a note of transient beauty.

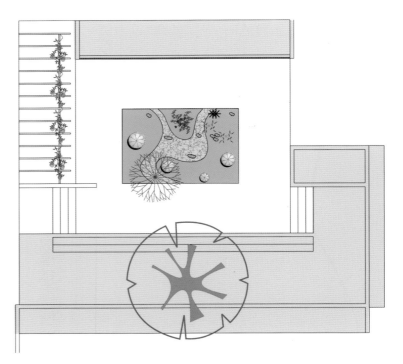

trees & palms	Camellia japonica	groundcover	climbers
Acer palmatum	Juniperus horizontalis	Dietes bicolor	Bouganvillea spectabilis
Magnolia x soulangeana	Phyllostachys pubescens	Duranta repens	Hedera canariensis
Myrciaria cauliflora	Rhododendron simsii	Iris germanica	Syngonium podophyllum
shrubs & bamboos	Viburnum suspensum	Ophiogopon planiscapus 'Nigrescens'	Wisteria floribunda
Buxus sempervirens		Zoysia	

above left & right Faisal's concept for replacing the water feature with a fluid design using pebbles, carefully placed stones and considered planting draws on Oriental inspiration.

below The intense red blooms of the *Bougainvillea spectabilis* stand out against the stark white walls, almost submerged in the leafy tree canopy.
left & bottom In his original design for the garden, Faisal created an organically shaped reflecting pool softened by abundant planting, including the iris-like *Dietes iridioides*, red *Rhododendron simsii* and aquatic plants in the water.

Large wooden steps offset in a diagonal line lead across the reflecting water to a breakfast patio that seems completely surrounded by nature.

02 piracaia garden

eduardo luppi | designer

location | bragança paulista

Set in a landscape of great natural beauty, water is present in every corner of this country garden near São Paulo. A large pond occupying one part of the land once belonged to the Piracaia water barrier, and was the only artificial element inherited by the property owners. When Eduardo Luppi was invited to visit the site with a view to developing the garden, he was excited by the clients' brief: to create a design in which water seemed to envelop the house. Luppi had already researched the qualities of water as a material and developed several techniques for using it in projects around the area, but the central challenge here was integrating the design with the dramatic natural landscape.

Luppi's vision of water as the transitional component between the garden and the landscape could not be more assertive, allowing the formation of volumes and creating sound near the house. The idea became reality in the form of a large pool adjacent to the building, the culmination of a series of small circular ponds built further down the sloping site. The water gently cascades down the gradient, as if trying to join the Piracaia water barrier beyond.

One of the most innovative aspects of the project is the use of large planters inside the reflecting pool. Luppi drilled holes around the planters to allow the water to circulate, and wrapped them with a Geotec membrane to prevent the earth from escaping through the holes. To add interest to the design and to prevent the soil being washed away he covered the surface of the pots with local cobbles.

Such attention to detail is apparent throughout the garden, which also draws on ideas from his own Japanese background, mixing pots with stones, aquatic plants and colourful fish. The French clients initially requested that the entire garden be planted with tropical and exotic plants. The flowing lines of the water mixed with lush foliage were favoured over the classical formal layout and plants of the French landscape, although ultimately Luppi did include clipped evergreens, including *Buxus sempervirens* (box), *Ligustrum* and conifers at the clients' suggestion.

Inside the pond Luppi created a simple composition of such aquatic plants as *Eichhornia crassipes* (water hyacinth), *Pistia stratiotes*, *Cyperus papyrus* (papyrus) and various species of water lilies (*Nymphaea*). Near the veranda, a small circular stone patio, big enough for a table and chairs, is the perfect place for breakfast, lunch or drinks. Wooden stepping slabs that appear to float in the water cross the pond to reach it. Sitting here, one can appreciate the surroundings and the scent of the *Spathodea*'s orange flowers, the pink and lilac of the stunning quaresmeira trees (*Tibouchina granulosa*), and the greenery of the large lawn and palm trees. For all who experience it, this is a place to become completely absorbed into the landscape.

above A drawing by C. Nkala shows clearly the main volumes of the garden: the pool almost wraps around the house and from it water cascades down the hill to a pond. Wooden steps connect the veranda to the small circular patio.

opposite below Edged by natural stone matched by the tones of the materials used in the circular patio area, the large pool finds echoes in the other water features and the landscape beyond, in a magnificent panorama of hills, sky and water.

trees & palms
Chamaecyparis lawsoniana
Phoenix roebelenii
Spathodea
Tibouchina granulosa

shrubs
Buxus sempervirens
Eugenia sprengelii
Ixora coccinea
Ligustrum sinense

Rhododendron indicum

groundcover
Dietes bicolor
Zantedeschia aethiopica

aquatic
Cyperus alternifolius
Cyperus papyrus
Eichhornia crassipes
Nymphaea caerulea
Pistia stratiotes

left Several species of aquatic plants and the graceful *Cyperus papyrus* blend harmoniously with the abundant native flora. The papyrus is growing in a submerged planter.
right A watercolour drawing by C. Nkala illustrates Luppi's concept for the garden.

opposite The simple lines of the farmhouse's modern Colonial architecture cohere with the bold approach of Eduardo Luppi's design.

above Water cascades from the pool next to the house towards small circular ponds further down, oxygenating the water and creating pleasing sounds.

Different textures and colours, lush planting and three cascades of water combine to create a dramatic effect. The inverted pyramidal planters are used as punctuation between stones laid in contrasting patterns.

03 atlante plaza

luiz vieira | designer
location | recife

A landscape project conceived as a piece of theatre, Luiz Vieira's design for the lobby of the Atlanta Plaza hotel undeniably succeeds in creating a sense of drama and surprise. This five-star hotel, designed by architect José Goiana Leal, stands magnificently facing the sea in Recife, capital of the state of Pernambuco in northeastern Brazil, in the city's most glamorous setting – the Boa Viagem Avenue.

With its striking façade and glowing, blue-lit exterior lift the hotel attracts the attention of tourists and passers-by. And immediately on entering at ground-floor level, visitors are confronted by a spectacular sculptural panel, 12 metres high and 40 metres long, running the entire length of the lobby. Fixed to the wall at an angle to allow better drainage for the lush planting that covers it, the panel is transformed into a vertical garden. And to create even more impact Vieira designed three stunning water cascades constructed from natural stone.

Delicate hand-made tiles by local artist Francisco Brennand cover panels on the surface of the wall, interspersed with inverted pyramidal planters clad in irregular white ceramic tiles and modules of the planting medium *xaxim*. A local rock – Itacolomi do Norte – is laid in the *canjiquinha* fashion of narrow horizontal strips. The interplay of the different elements, rough and smooth, natural and man-made, creates a sophisticated composition of colours and textures. Individual elements are made slightly curved, breaking the rigidity of the overall geometric shape, and echoing the waves of the sea just beyond the hotel door.

Each of the water cascades has a unique character, while complementing the others to create a unified whole. The main cascade is skilfully constructed using large *inhame* stones to resemble a natural waterfall. Granite blocks laid horizontally achieve a softer effect in the other cascades, as the water flows into the lower reflecting pools, finally merging in a large tank that links the internal and external spaces of the hotel through the glass façade of the building. A vertical fountain in the entrance mirrors an external water feature.

Tropical planting seems to grow naturally from the wall and is divided into distinct groupings: a strong vertical element is provided by the tall stems and umbrella-like leaves of *Cyperus alternifolius*; in the hanging *xaxim* blocks are several kinds of orchids; and the luxuriant climbers *Monstera deliciosa* and *Scindapsus aureus* scramble up to a height of 10 metres.

Clients and designer were delighted with both the functional and aesthetic affects achieved by the panel and the integration of the lobby with the main entrance. But the most appreciative comments come from hotel visitors, who constantly remark on the pleasing environment and the songs of the birds that took up residence during construction of the wall and now build their nests there.

palms

Chrysalidocarpus
   lutescens

Euterpe oleracea

Ptychosperma elegans

shrubs

Brassaia actinophylla

Dicksonia fibrosa

Philodendron
   undulatum

groundcover

Alpinia purpurata

Calathea lancifolia

Dieffenbachia
   amoena

Schizocentron elegans

Spathiphyllum
   commutatum

Philodendron
   oxycardium

Nephrolepis
   biserfurcans

climbers

Monstera deliciosa

Scindapsus aureus

aquatics

Cyperus alternifolius

above & below Plan and elevation of the Atlante Plaza lobby show how the cascades and pools, planting and structural materials, all work together in this adventurous and fantastical work.

opposite Seated in the hotel bar, guests can appreciate the sound of water, the luxuriousness of the planting and the drama of the sculptural wall.

One of the existing rustic cottages sits comfortably next to the grandeur of a waterfall in a relaxed relationship.

04 the oriental influence

barbara uccello & maringa pilz | designers
location | ilhabela

Ilhabela, near São Sebastião in the southeast of Brazil, is a true paradise. And on the edge of the island's mountains, close to the sea, Barbara Uccello and Maringa Pilz created this exciting, exotic garden, covering over 20,000 square metres. An abundance of water and three old fishermen's cottages came with the property; the architecture, in the local vernacular style, is intimate yet airy, comfortable but elegant.

The two designers found instant inspiration in the family's travels to the Orient. 'The clients loved nature and tropical vegetation and requested from us flowering species of our tropical flora, as well as plants from countries such as Thailand, Indonesia and Polynesia. They also wanted water to be present in the garden.' It was a brief that suited the designers perfectly, as they had developed their own style by travelling and studying in countries such as Japan, Bali, China, India and Tahiti, as well as Brazil. 'Our inspiration comes from the elements of our country such as bamboo, stones, the tones of sky and sea; also the strong colours of our arts and crafts, the spirit of the place, the endless sunny days, the hues of the little boats, and above all, our tropical vegetation and the wealth of our diversity.'

In order to incorporate all their various ideas, Uccello and Pilz drew up a master plan and undertook a detailed study of the existing vegetation. While the location was beautiful, it was rustic and undeveloped, and on the whole lacked colourful flowers. Involved in all aspects of the project, the designers also suggested ideas for the refurbishment of the houses, introducing colours and materials such as bamboo and straw, and proposing several pools on different levels. Bridges and seats made of aroeira wood allow people to gaze out over the landscape and listen to the sound of water. The architecture perfectly matches the Ilhabela lifestyle and the vegetation is in complete harmony with the sky, mountains and sea.

As each phase of the garden was completed, the designers moved on to the next, creating multiple tiny gardens that slowly built up to form this large masterpiece. The waterfalls and natural swimming pools are a major feature. An apparently conventional swimming pool reveals on closer inspection a surprise: a large outcrop of rock sits surreally on the bottom. Found during the excavation of the pool, it was incorporated into the finished design. As well as an intriguing visual device, the stone warms the water by conserving heat during the day. Swimming there in the evening as the sun sets is an unforgettable experience. Another spectacular place to bathe is a waterfall enjoying views out over the landscape.

Planting connects and also creates privacy for each house, with height and interest provided by flowering and fruit trees such as *Triplaris brasiliensis*, *Amherstia nobilis*, the Flamboyant tree (*Delonix regia*) and the *ipê* or Trumpet tree (*Tabebuia*). Shrubs including *Nerium oleander* and *Thunbergia erecta* bring colour closer to eye level. Groundcover plants attract attention downwards, with blue agapanthus and bright yellow hemerocallis, while climbers such as bougainvillea and jasmine add colour, scent and romance to this island paradise.

far left A table and benches made from uncut timber form strong horizontals in front of the towering vertical bamboos.
left The gorgeous bloom of *Amherstia nobilis*, often known as the Queen of Flowering Trees.
below Wood, bamboo, stones, reeds – and water – are some of the natural elements incorporated into the garden.
opposite A wooden bridge connects one house with another, crossing dramatic waterfalls.

trees & palms
Amherstia nobilis
Anacardium occidentale
Artocarpus incisa
Brownea sp.
Caryota mitis
Delonix regia
Erythrina crista-galli
Erythrina mulungu
Jacaranda caroba
Lecythis pisonis
Liculuala sp.
Magnolia x soulangeana
Mangifera indica
Psidium guajava
Plumeria rubra
Spathodea sp.
Stenocalyx pitanga
Tabebuia avellanedae
Triplaris brasiliensis

shrubs
Agave americana
Bauhinia galpinii
Clerodendron sp.
Mussaenda sp.
Nerium oleander
Punica granatum
Thunbergia erecta

groundcover
Agapanthus africanus
Aloe sp.
Alpinia purpurata
Crinum erubescens
Crinum procerum
Heliconia psittacorum
Heliconia rostrata
Hemerocallis flava
Strelitzia reginae
Vriesea imperialis

climbers
Bougainvillea spectabilis
Ipomoea sp.
Jasminum nitidum
Saritaea magnifica
Strongylodon macrobotrys
Wisteria floribunda

aquatics
Cyperus papyrus

above Wooden decking, stone and grass create a natural setting for the swimming pool, with an unexpected rock outcrop at the bottom.

right Inspiration for this remarkable garden was drawn from a number of sources: the pervasive presence of water, the colours and materials found in the local environment and the clients' travels to the Orient.

opposite An Oriental-style container planted with the palm *Licuala* and the feathery light foliage of *Cyperus papyrus* offer further hints of foreign places.

In an organically flowing line, the edge of the pool reaches out to encircle an existing palm tree.

05 an organic pool

gil fialho | designer

location | siriuba

From this private beach house in Siriuba, on the island of Ilhabela, spectacular views extend across long, broad waterways and sweeping mountains – the forms of which are mirrored in the organic shapes of pools and paths in the garden designed by Gil Fialho. In a natural and relaxed interplay between architecture and landscape, everything is eye-catching and invites the viewer on a series of fascinating journeys.

Located in what were once the grounds of an old hotel, now demolished, this exceptional landscape project extends over 10,000 square metres. When Fialho initially inspected the site, his first concern was how to incorporate the natural water resources of the property into his design. The striking curves of the mountains of the Serra do Mar and the exuberance of the Atlantic forest are also absorbed into this first-rate garden blueprint.

Fialho took advantage of several existing springs towards the bottom of a hill to create a still water feature, as well as a swimming pool with a gentle, organic shape. In addition to providing the right conditions for a collection of aquatic and marsh-dwelling plants, the water feature also retains and slows excess runoff during the region's summer rainstorms. The swimming pool too serves both a practical and an aesthetic function, with its organic lines reaching out to encircle an existing palm tree.

A curving deck on the terrace in front of the house appears rustic, as if it had been there for decades, an effect Fialho achieved by treating the wood with a chlorine solution. Elsewhere, both to keep costs down and to ensure that the materials are in complete harmony with the location, stones found during construction were used in paths, pool, walks and retaining walls.

Contrary to what is often assumed, Brazilian gardens are not exclusively full of displays of vibrantly coloured flowers. In this project, green – punctuated by bursts of colour – is dominant, strengthened by a confident use of architectural plants to give structure. Fialho selected plants with distinctive shapes as a visual device, and also to attract the enormous diversity of birds and insects in this environmental conservation area.

Around the house exotic forms and flowers frame and clothe the architecture. Climbers soften the lines of the building and provide more privacy to the rooms inside. In areas exposed to the strong northwest wind, wind-resistant plants such as philodendrons and hardy palm trees are used. For shadier corners several heliconias and plants from the *Marantaceae* family form long drifts to enhance the natural topography. And in the water feature Fialho planted the stunning and unusual *Typhonodorum lindleyanum*, which rises like a natural sculpture. Far from the house, almost at the boundaries of the property, a glimpse of an orchard of delicious tropical fruit trees sets us off on a new journey of discovery.

trees & palms
Areca triandra
Caryota mitis
Cassia fistula
Chrysalidocarpus lutescens
Clerodendron thomsoniae
Clusia fluminensis
Cocos nucifera
Delonix regia
Latania lontaroides
Licuala grandis
Malvaviscus arboreus

Myrciaria cauliflora
Neodypsis decary
Pandanus utilis
Phoenix roebelenii
Pinanga kuhli
Thrinax parviflora
Washingtonia filifera
shrubs & bamboos
Bambusa multiplex
Bambusa vulgaris var. aureo-
   marginata
Brunfelsia uniflora

Carissa macrocarpa
Clerodendron speciosissimum
Cordyline indivisa
Dicksonia sellowiana
Gardenia jasminoides
Hibiscus pernambucensis
Hibiscus rosa-sinensis
Leea coccinea
Medinilla magnifica
Musa coccinea
Musa sumatra
Mussaenda erythrophylla

Mussaenda incana
Odontonema strictum
Phyllostachys aurea
Pleomele reflexa
Ravenala madagascariensis
Russelia equisetiformis
Sanchezia nobilis
Tetrapanax papyriferum
Thunbergia erecta
groundcover
Aglaonema commutatum
Alocasia cucullata

Alocasia macrorrhiza
Alpinia purpurata
Alpinia sanderae
Ananas bracteatus
Anthurium sp.
Aphelandra sinclairiana
Asplenium nidus
Calathea roseo-picta
Colocasia gigantea
Costus speciosus
Costus spiralis
Crinum erubescens
Curculigo capitulata
Ctenanthe
  oppenheimiana
Cyclanthus bipartitus
Dietes vegeta
Duranta repens
Evolvulus glomeratus
Heliconia angusta
Heliconia collinsiana
Heliconia episcopalis
Heliconia x rauliniana
Heliconia rostrata
Heliconia stricta
Hemerocallis flava
Justicia brandegeana
Lysimachia congestiflora
Maranta sp.
Maranta zebrina
Neomarica caerulea
Pandanus baptistii
Philodendron meliononi
Philodendron undulatum
Pilea cadierei
Rhoeo discolor
Spatiphyllum cannifolium
Spathiphyllum wallisii
Strelitzia augusta
Strelitzia reginae
Tapeinochilus ananassae
Tradescantia zebrina
Turnera ulmifolia
Zingiber zerumbet

climbers

Abutilon megapotamicum
Allamanda cathartica
Allamanda violacea
Bougainvillea glabra
Congea tomentosa
Ipomoea sp.
Monstera deliciosa
Nicolaia elatior
Philodendron martianum
Philodendron selloum
Plumbago capensis

Podreana ricasoliana
Scindapsus aureus
Strongylodon macrobotrys
Syngonium podophyllum
Thunbergia mysorensis

aquatics

Cyperus papyrus
Nymphaea sp.
Typhonodorum lindleyanum

opposite Rooftops and terraces are glimpsed from above through the intriguing shapes of the trunks and foliage of trees and the massed architectural plants.

opposite The water feature is home to luxuriant aquatic plants, including the sculptural *Typhonodorum lindleyanum*.
left Trees and climbers frame and clothe the built structures. Shades of green are dominant, lightened by splashes of colour.
below The curving decking in front of the house echoes the lines of other man-made structures in the garden, as well as the mountains beyond.

far left Water jets in the stone wall behind the pool create a peaceful sound during the warm sunny days. **left & below** Kfouri inserted the pool in a space between the apartment building and the urban street. Vertiginous aerial views reveal the abstract design created in blue tiles, with the curvilinear forms intercepted by the formal straight lines of decking. In the centre is a single specimen of *Plumeria rubra*.

06 diving into abstraction

jamil jose kfouri | designer
location | são paolo

When Jamil Jose Kfouri was invited to design this landscape, the Irataua building – another modernist skyscraper in São Paulo's concrete jungle – was already in place in this exclusive residential area. The architects had left an irregular-shaped site in an uncompromisingly urban context, close to Ibirapuera, one of São Paulo's largest and most popular parks. Streets crossed one side of the plot while natural vegetation remained on the other.

Unusually for São Paulo, where gardens generally face inwards, Kfuori's garden is largely planned to face out to the existing vegetation and towards the urban street. However, the street trees worked as strong backdrop for the designer's proposed ideas: a pergola, a barbecue area, a playground and a swimming pool.

Kfuori positioned the pergola and barbecue in a more private and peaceful area, providing the occupants of the building with shade on sunny days and a space to invite friends and family for food and drinks. Children can enjoy the playground, situated under the pergola, and from this area of the garden everyone can watch the games of squash being played inside the building.

But it is the arresting swimming pool, inspired by the wacky and curvilinear shapes of Burle Marx's designs, that forms the main focus of the project. Positioned in the sunniest part of the garden, it is lined with tiles in different shades of blue laid in abstract patterns that produce a dazzling visual effect. Behind the pool is a stone wall built of rough blocks in a soothing earthy colour. Water jets installed in the wall add interest and the dimension of sound for the swimmers and sunbathers. On the other side is an area of honey-coloured decking whose straight, parallel lines and rectilinear form cut into the strong curves of the swimming pool. Residents of the apartment block and high-living neighbours have vertiginous aerial views of this spectacular abstract feature of the garden.

Seating clad in brilliant white marble – a stone used both inside and outside the building – contrasts with other materials, including wood, pink marble and granite. More traditional wooden benches are placed next to the swimming pool and around raised beds and tranquil pools of reflecting water. A meandering path around the garden uses the same Portuguese mosaic immortalized in Burle Marx's Copacabana beach pavement.

Kfouri deliberately kept the planting simple. Designed to be appropriate to each of the garden's specific areas, it consists mostly of low shrubs and perennials to keep the views open. Specimens of the giant bromeliad *Vriesea imperialis* form compositions with boulders and pebbles, while the pampas grass *Cortaderia selloana*, with its tufts of spiky leaves and fluffy heads, provides contrast in both colour and texture. The key plant throughout the garden is the decorative tree *Plumeria rubra* (frangipani) – a single specimen of which forms a focal point in the pool decking – filling the garden with its heavenly fragrance as it blooms in the summer months.

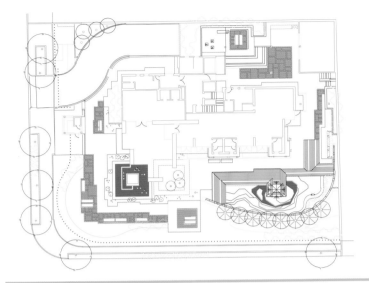

trees & palms	shrubs & bamboos	groundcover	Spathiphyllum sp.
Brassaia actinophylla	Arundinaria japonica	Agapanthus orientalis	Vriesea imperialis
Callistemon viminalis	Bambusa gracilis	Alpinia nutans	Zoysia
Erythrina speciosa	Gardenia jasminoides	Ananas bracteatus	**climbers**
Euterpe edulis	Ixora coccinea	Arachis sp.	Parthenocissus tricuspidata
Pandanus utilis	Ligustrum lucidum	Cortaderia selloana	Philodendron martianum
Pinanga kuhli	'Aureovariegatum'	Lantana camara	Philodendron oxycardium
Plumeria rubra	Nandina domestica	Moraea bicolor	Plumbago capensis
Rhapis excelsa	Phormium tenax	Philodendron melinonii	
Tabebuia chrysotricha	'Variegatum'	Russelia equisetiformis	
		Schizocentron elegans	

top right Kfouri used traditional seating in the form of wooden benches around the pool terrace, contrasting with the ultra-modern, clean lines of the pool itself.

above, left to right & opposite below From every angle, the dazzling abstract design in blue tiles can be seen through the rippling transparency of the pool's surface.

opposite above left A barbecue area in a more secluded area of the garden allows the residents to enjoy outdoor living in this communal project.

opposite above right The bold leaf shapes of the giant bromeliad *Vriesea imperialis* look magnificent against cool white marble and natural pebbles.

Palm fronds create intriguing
shadow shapes on the almost
glacial white paving, which forms
a continuous level with the mirrored
surface of the pool.

07 mirror by the sea

sergio menon | designer
location | **iporanga**

An ideal of architecture in harmony with nature was the starting point for this project, a collaboration between a celebrated architect, the late Cláudio Bernardes, and a talented garden designer, Sergio Menon. Bernardes was famous for being virtually the only professional in his field concerned with this architectural dialogue, a genuinely Brazilian stylist who translated the materials and shapes of the local landscape into lines of striking simplicity and functionality. The house, a beach property in Iporanga, in the resort of Guarujá near São Paulo, is set in the luxuriant Atlantic forest and encircled by mountains.

In the garden, Menon set out to observe the natural proportions of the landscape, with its sensual contours and volumes, creating a design that is completely in keeping with the house and that echoes its surroundings. The sea is a constant presence that also had to be acknowledged and accommodated in the design. Reached through the relaxed and modern house, the garden is built on three generous levels on land that slopes gently down towards the water.

The client, an architect himself, asked for an exuberant garden to surround the house, stressing the need for privacy from other properties in this residential development. Menon accentuated the change of levels and picked out the lines and materials used in the architecture, so that the garden participates with both the house and the wider setting. This is apparent, for instance, in the lawn stretching between the swimming pool and the beach, following a clear trajectory from the house to the edge of the property.

The pool and its terrace are severe, but serenely elegant, clad in sheets of natural travertine marble, each one metre square. When not disturbed by bathers, the surface of the water is a tranquil mirror, calmly reflecting the surrounding landscapes. The smooth marble surface around the pool creates a platform to display the outdoor decoration. In this area the planting was kept fairly simple, with a sculptural double-trunked *Beaucarnea* enhanced by the beautiful medium-sized *Phoenix* palms.

Menon's bold use of architectural and exotic plants, including those of Asiatic origin, such as heliconia, bromeliads, orchids and palms, creates an autonomous garden while successfully merging it with the Atlantic forest beyond, giving the impression that the local environment, in its intrinsic beauty, has been respected and left unaltered. In one single, integrated concept, the transparency of the house completely immerses it in the sense of nature created in the garden.

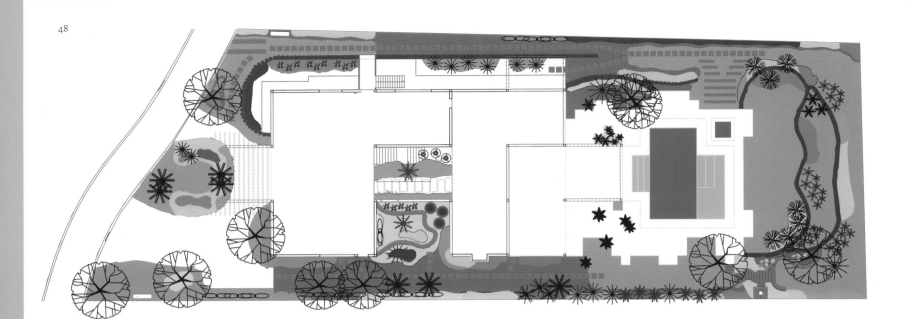

trees & palms	shrubs & bamboos	groundcover	
Areca triandra	Aechmea aquilega	Alpinia purpurata	Ophiopogon jaburan
Beaucarnea recurvata	Agave americana	Alpinia zerumbet	Ophiopogon japonicus
Caryota mitis	Agave angustifolia	Ananas bracteatus	Pandanus baptistii
Clusia fluminensis	Arundina bambusifolia	Asparagus densiflorus	Pandanus racemosus
Dypsis decaryi	Cycas revoluta	Asparagus sp.	Philodendron bipinnatifidum
Eugenia uniflora	Gardenia jasminoides	Belamcamda chinensis	Pilea nummulariifolia
Hyophorbe verschaffeltii	Ixora coccinea compacta	Callisia repens	Strelitzia augusta
Pandanus utilis	Leea rubra	Heliconia psittacorum	Strelitzia reginae
Phoenix roebelenii	Phormium tenax	Heliconia rostrata	Tradescantia zebrina
Pritchardia pacifica	Pleomele reflexa	Liriope muscari	Zoysia japonica
Ravenala madagascariensis	Thunbergia erecta	Moraea bicolor	Zoysia tenuifolia
Roystonea regia		Neomarica caerulea	**climber**
Veitchia merrillii			Bougainvillea spectabilis
Washingtonia filifera			

above The landscape begins inside the house, where Menon planted a tall *Pandanus* and verdant vegetation beside the path leading out into the garden.

right Planting around the swimming pool is kept fairly simple, with a double-trunked *Beaucarnea recurvata* forming a focal point. The house can be opened up to the garden as required.

opposite below left Travertine marble paving is a perfect hardscaping material to effect the smooth transition between swimming pool and lawn.

opposite below centre From the house there is a stunning view of the coastline and the sea, the mountains and the native beach vegetation.

opposite below right In this successful collaboration between architect Claudio Bernardes and garden designer Sergio Menon, the lines of the house are seamlessly integrated with the garden and the natural landscape beyond.

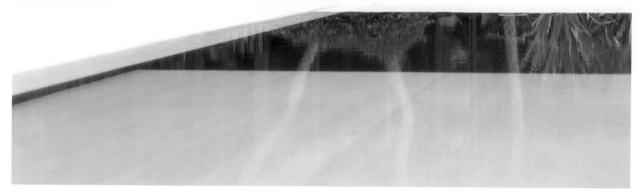

right The amazing swimming pool seems just a step away from the sea. It can be used for play or exercise, but is also a tranquil mirror reflecting the sky and surrounding landscapes.

opposite left above Close to the house stepping stones lead out into the garden. Planting here uses a variety of different-textured groundcover as well as palms and *Pandanus* for height and verticality.

opposite left centre Ravenalas and other tropical plants make an unusual and effective exotic hedge, protecting the client from the neighbouring properties.

opposite left below Railway sleepers as steps are one of the many informal hardscaping materials used around the garden.

opposite right Broad and elegant, the travertine marble terrace is enhanced by the green of the tropical foliage. Furniture is placed strategically at the side entrance of the garden, for the clients to sit and relax, overlooking the beautiful landscape.

The undulating coastline of Guarujá is the perfect backdrop to the curving infinity of the pool.

08 an infinite pool

evani kuperman franco | designer

location | guarujá

The Tijucupava garden is a dream space where different water surfaces meet in the infinite, where nature cohabits happily with man-made architectural elements and planted vegetation blends harmoniously with local flora. Located in the seaside area of Guarujá, the garden is built amid the magnificent Atlantic forest in a private ecological reserve. Architect Carlos Zeibel Costa designed a house with wide openings and generous terraces facing the sea in a curvilinear design that follows the coastline. This design allows free circulation between spaces, creating a physical and visual unity with nature. Mixing natural and artificial materials and the maritime and forest environments, the house successfully integrates inside with outside.

To achieve the required result in the landscape, designer Evani Kuperman Franco combined hard landscape materials and charismatic vegetation. For the planting strategy Kuperman wanted to create an atmosphere of intimacy between existing and new vegetation. Plants such as *Vriesea imperialis*, *Agave angustifolia*, *Yucca filamentosa*, *Pandanus utilis* and *Dietes bicolor* add diversity, texture and colour to the scheme and create a composition as lively as the Atlantic itself, while ensuring the diversity of the planting does not conflict with the existing surroundings.

The hardscaping uses natural materials such as São Thome stone, which resembles the tonality of beach sand and contrasts well with the green of the vegetation. The pergola, made of recycled eucalyptus structural members and bamboo roofing, is the main three-dimensional element of the project and its lateral screen works as an artistic background. A long table made of polar-white granite is used for presenting food and drink for guests during the long warm and sunny days.

On one side of the swimming pool, where the clients and their guests can appreciate the interplay of different water surfaces, decking is made of recycled pine. The pool's blue mosaic echoes the colour of the sea and accentuates the perception that it extends into the infinite. At night discreet fibre-optic lighting maintains this close relationship between the water's reflection on the clear bright nights and the pool, ensuring that the garden is a magical and ethereal landscape.

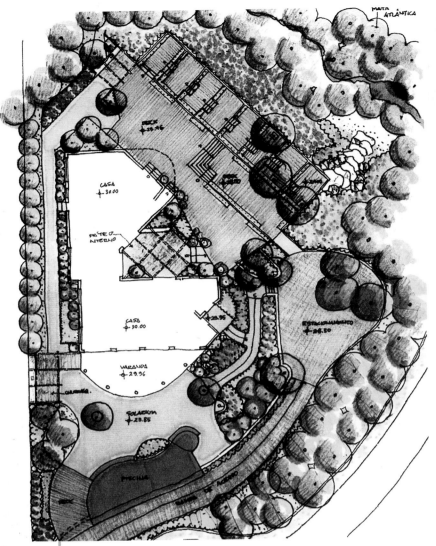

trees & palms

Caryota mitis

Clusia fluminensis

Cocos nucifera

Eugenia uniflora

Licuala grandis

Pandanus utilis

Phoenix roebelenii

Pinanga kuhlii

Rhapis excelsa

Syagrus romanzoffiana

shrubs & bamboos

Acalypha reptans

Agave angustifolia

Bambusa gracilis

Clerodendron thomsoniae

Hibiscus rosa-sinensis

Ixora coccinea

Musa paradisiaca

Phormium tenax

Phyllostachys pubescens

Pleomele reflexa

Ravenala madagascariensis

Yucca filamentosa

groundcover

Alpinia purpurata

Asparagus densiflorus

Axonopus compressus

Catharanthus roseus

Costus erythrophyllus

Cuphea gracilis

Dietes bicolor

Echeveria elegans

Evolvulus sp.

Hedychium coronarium

Heliconia caribaea

Heliconia collinsiana

Impatiens walleriana

Nicolaia elatior

Ophiopogon japonicus

Peperomia scandens

Philodendron bipinnatifidum

Pilea cadierei

Pilea nummulariifolia

Portulaca grandiflora

Strelitizia alba

Tradescantia spathacea

Tradescantia zebrina
 'Purpusii'

Vriesea imperialis

Zoysia japonica

climbers

Allamanda cathartica

Bougainvillea spectabilis

Ficus pumila 'Variegata'

Monstera deliciosa

Passiflora alata

Pereskia aculeata

Philodendron undulatum

Plumbago capensis

Rhaphidophora decursiva

aquatics

Cyperus alternifolius

Cyperus papyrus

page 54 A pergola constructed from uprights of eucalyptus trunks and slatted bamboo takes on a different appearance – and different functions – by day and at night.

page 55 Loose-decked platforms cascade down the site's gradient, leaving the vegetation untouched. The rigidity of white-painted pine boards contrasts with the trees that break its surface.

above Essentially a semicircle, the pool mediates between the house's architecture and the loosely flowing seaside. Hardscaping includes decking and stone elements.

right At night proximity and distance blur as discreet lighting creates a completely different atmosphere.

left & above Planting along the path to the swimming pool includes a fantastic diversity of vegetation, whose shapes and colour are in harmony with the Atlantic forest's charismatic flora. The bold leaves of *Vrisea imperialis* contrast with the thinner verticals of *Dietes bicolor*, the *Pandanus utilis* is used as a focal point in the border, and the transparency of the feathery *Cyperus papyrus* filters the blue of the sea.

planting

planting

The value of the plant in the composition, like the value of colour in paintings, is always relative. The plant is made valuable by the contrast or harmony created by its relation to the other plants.

Roberto Burle Marx

Plants and planting are central to any discussion of gardens, and perhaps Brazilian gardens in particular. Architectural shapes and exotic colours are ubiquitous, whether in the fabulously large leaves of the banana or the strong verticals of palm trees such as *Phoenix* and *Ravenala*. Electric pinks of bougainvillea clash and contrast with the red and yellow of the Flamboyant (*Delonix*) and *ipê* (*Tabebuia*) trees found throughout Brazil. But tones don't always have to be hot and vibrant – cool green, in a variety of textures, can calm things down, or create a subtle transition between more colourful plants.

In today's Brazilian landscape garden, planting is defiantly eclectic: from the topiary and manicured formality of the French tradition; to the wild, jungly style echoing the native forest, with its oversized leaves and tall plants; or the popular Japanese fashion, which mixes tropical plants in an asymmetrical, restrained design.

But all styles pay homage in one way or another to the legacy of Roberto Burle Marx. What once was seen as innovative – Burle Marx's flowing lines mixed with large swathes of colourful plants – is now absorbed into the tradition. Burle Marx, of course, also made use of other natural materials – stones, cobbles, mosaics and even the earth itself. His combination of a strong, new aesthetic philosophy with an endless curiosity about the plant world is totally distinctive.

And all styles also reflect the wealth of Brazil's flora, both native and imported, its natural strong sunlight and the shapes of the magnificent mountains. Today, Brazil undoubtedly has a number of very creative professionals and a wealth of plants that can potentially be used in the garden and landscape.

Gardens where planting is the main element are featured in this chapter. In the first part, planting in the city, Guilhermina Machado shows what can be achieved with a limited palette of striking vegetation in a garden by the sea. Bold planting can also be romantic, as seen in Iza Vieira Ruprecht's design for a garden in São Paulo. A project where European and tropical ideas exist in harmony is found in Orlando Busarello's travellers' garden. Adventurous planting against a restrained background marks Anna Maria Prado Dantas's design for a project begun by Burle Marx, while a walk in Isabel Duprat's BankBoston headquarters provides a glimpse of today's innovative Brazilian public space. Planting in the country reveals another approach, as the Alto da Boa Vista farm, also by Duprat, demonstrates how to work with exuberant surroundings. Planting on a large canvas, where the colour of the plants was applied as if the garden was a painting, is found in the three valleys by Sonia Infante. In Minas Gerais, you can be surprised by an oasis of tropical plants designed by Luiz Carlos Orsini and dazzled by the flamboyant and colourful planting of Marcelo Novaes's garden in the country.

previous pages The Three Valleys (p. 95).
left Influenced by the coastal situation and climate, Alex Hanazaki created a tropical seaside garden for this house, characterized by strong planting schemes. Here, striking rosettes of imperial bromeliads bask in the sun next to the dappled shade cast by a pergola built of macandaruba wood, host to the bright red climber bougainvillea. In spite of the great diversity, the attention with which each plant was selected and placed in the garden is evident, a result of a careful study of plant shapes and forms so that each does not conflict with the others.

opposite Different hues of green and an eclectic mix of shapes, form and texture were used in this design by Isabel Duprat to create a plant composition rich in interest. In the background the existing vegetation contrasts with the palm *Ptychosperma macarthuri* used as an accent plant.
below Abstract planting is perhaps the most appropriate way of describing Luiz Carlos Orsini's design for this modern residence in Belo Horizonte, Minas Gerais. Beaucarneas used in groups partially cloak the house and the bromeliad *Neoregelia* 'Fireball' was planted under them, forming a red carpet. Both house and planting are reflected in the swimming pool.

Exuberant planting consisting of *Cycas revoluta* and *Pleomele reflexa* seems to explode next to the house. Each plant has a different texture and shape, but Machado allowed enough space for their strong personalities to be expressed.

01 planting by the sea

guilhermina machado | designer

location | barra da tijuca

Rio de Janeiro spreads its wings in a seemingly endless embrace around the coast, and one element in this ever-expanding urban stretch is Barra da Tijuca. A new residential area, it is highly sought after by the wealthy, artists and others who are in search of a more peaceful lifestyle, far from the frenetic pace of Copacabana and Ipanema. Low-rise buildings, large, private condominiums and huge mansions make up this neighbourhood, where quiet prevails in the shade of the Flamboyant and *ipê* trees which gracefully scatter their red and yellow petals on the roads that all lead to one place – the sea.

Not far from the shore is this beautiful garden designed by Guilhermina Machado on a site covering 2,400 square metres. In the initial stage of the project, Machado removed the rampant weeds and unwanted vegetation left behind after the house was completed, but incorporated into her preliminary ideas precious existing trees. These included coconuts and three *Geriba* palms, as well as two large and spectacular Flamboyant trees (*Delonix regia*) that stand majestically against the sky, giving height and instant maturity to the project. The clients themselves already had an exceptional knowledge of plants, but they gave Machado freedom in her choice of planting – as long as she used interesting and high-quality specimens.

Apart from the swimming pool and patio, areas of hard landscaping are almost entirely absent from this garden. Circulation is guided by natural stepping stones that gently lead to the pool and around the garden. House and veranda are surrounded by a large expanse of lawn, punctuated by the skilful and deceptively simple planting that is the hallmark of this design – restrained in the use of different varieties but exuberant in its individual elements.

Vibrant splashes of colour light up the area near the pool, where Machado placed pots containing the bird-of-paradise flower, *Strelitzia reginae*, along with hibiscus and hemerocallis. The climber *Trachelospermum jasminoides* covers a wall and scents the garden during long summer evenings with its white flowers. Strong foliage shapes are provided by *Dracaena marginata*, *Vriesea imperialis* and *Aechmea fasciata*.

In front of the house Machado created a distinctive composition consisting of the giant bromeliad *Vriesea imperialis* grouped around the palm *Phoenix roebelenii*, all framed by large natural boulders. Green is the predominant colour here, and so to add brightness, the white-flowered orchid *Phalaenopsis* was trained on the trunks of the palms.

Throughout the garden a sense of unity is achieved by using a limited palette of plants, but Machado ensures this does not become monotonous by occasionally introducing those with strong personalities, such as the tree fern *Dicksonia sellowiana*, *Cycas revoluta* and *Ficus benjamina*. Nothing was taken for granted in even the smallest corner of the garden, and it is this attention to detail, even when a simple composition is all that is required, that can make a garden exceptional.

trees & palms

Beaucarnea recurvata

Clusia fluminensis

Cocos nucifera

Delonix regia

Ficus benjamina

Geriba sp.

Licuala sp.

Phoenix roebelenii

shrubs & bamboos

Azalea sp.

Buxus sempervirens

Cycas circinalis

Cycas revoluta

Dicksonia sellowiana

Dracaena marginata

Dracaena reflexa

Hibiscus sp.

Ixora coccinea

Pleomele reflexa

Yucca aloifolia

groundcover

Aechmea fasciata

Alcantarea imperialis

Bromeliads

Chlorophytum comosum

Hemerocallis sp.

Lantana camara

Peperomia scandens

Schizocentron elegans

Spathiphyllum sp.

Strelitzia reginae

Vriesea imperialis

climbers & epiphytes

Ficus pumila

Phalaenopsis sp.

Platycerium sp.

Trachelospermum
 jasminoides

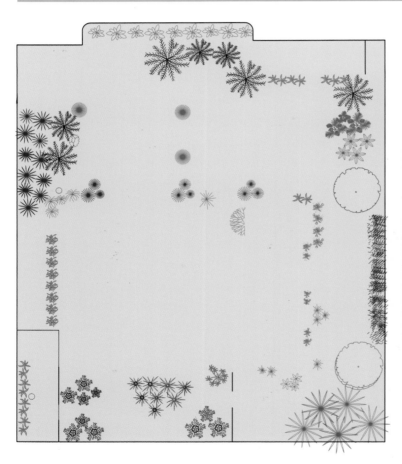

A large expanse of lawn, seen in a detail of Machado's plan, is enlivened by the remarkably inventive and luxuriant planting.

opposite & below The height of this composition comes from the already existing coconut tree, to which was added the palm *Phoenix roebelenii*, both underplanted with *Vriesea imperialis* in beds outlined with circles of large stones. To add brightness, the white-flowered orchid *Phalaenopsis* was trained on the trunk of the palms. The climber *Ficus pumila* clothes the wall and the bright red flowers of the Flamboyant tree (*Delonix regia*) seem to float above.

Railway sleepers used as steps are almost submerged in a sea of the black grass *Ophiopogon planiscapus* 'Nigrescens'. Ruprecht continued the use of the black grass on the level above, to instil rhythm and unity in the design. Colour comes from the *Cymbidium* orchids and the flowering trees.

02 a bold romantic garden

iza vieira ruprecht | designer
location | são paolo

For many designers, working on a garden on different levels can be a daunting challenge, requiring an experienced eye during site appreciation and survey. Every view has to be taken into consideration across the entire garden, to ensure that the design works at each level – and between them – and with plants at the right heights, to create a unified concept.

Iza Vieira Ruprecht developed this garden on sloping terrain in one of several of the new suburban areas of São Paulo, near the Guarapiranga dam. The house was built at the top of the site and was surrounded by a derelict garden extending to almost 4,000 square metres at the lower levels. Glass had been used extensively in the construction of the house, flooding it with light and bringing the garden closer to the occupants.

All the areas created by Ruprecht evolved instinctively from the shape of the land, with the garden following the rising and falling of the ground. Changes in level are achieved either by steps, using natural materials such as railway sleepers and stone, or, taking advantage of the slope, gentle ramps.

'The clients were keen on having flat and quiet areas,' Ruprecht notes, 'where they could read and meditate, as well as spending time relaxing with family and friends.' To meet this request, she designed a large stone terrace to provide a place to sit and view the entire space. From here, the peacock flowers of *Caesalpinia* and the gorgeous, exotic blooms of *Tibouchina mutabilis* and heliconias can be enjoyed, planted along the fence that runs to boundary of the property. Radiating out from the house and terrace, serpentine paths seem to flow around the garden, following its contours like water and making every part accessible.

In the main border, Ruprecht created a mandala out of an antique container, where still water collects. Birds come from the surrounding Atlantic forest to drink and take their daily bath, overlooked by a gigantic outcrop of rock called the 'pedra achatada', one of the local landmarks. Around this water feature is a large expanse of the black grass *Ophiopogon planiscapus* 'Nigrescens', together with *Cymbidium* orchids and *Pentas*, planted in a striking and rhythmic arrangement.

Spaces in this garden are intimate and contemplative, enhanced by the romantic and subtle planting and by the fact that the hard landscaping does not conflict with nature. Wherever you are in the garden, there is a feeling of being in the right place, whether walking under the shade of the mature trees or simply sitting on the benches placed strategically at various points, listening to bird song and enjoying the generous planting. Delicately scented flowers and delicious fruits add to the sensuous experience of the garden, restoring energy lost in daily life.

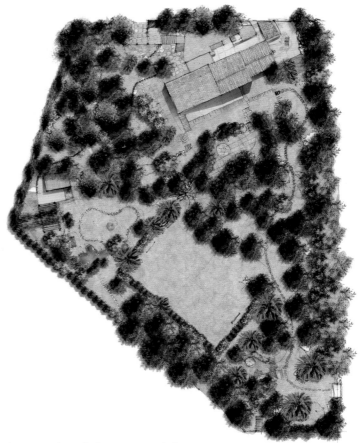

above In an angle of the veranda a tree trunk was adapted as a container for a stunning pink orchid. Abundant planting in the background includes the blossoms of *Brunfelsia uniflora*.

opposite top left Mature trees and romantically full planting create intimate spaces within the garden, but also allow glimpses of the landscape beyond.

opposite top right A simple still water feature in the form of a

mandala is planted around with the black grass *Ophiopogon* and beautiful and exotic orchids and *Pentas*, providing both colour and interest without overwhelming the sense of calm.

opposite below From the highest point of the land, where the house is situated, the garden unfolds on a steep slope. Skilful planting ensures interest at all levels – from groundcover to tall trees – and across

the site, without feeling overcrowded or claustrophobic. Ruprecht also ensured year-round interest of foliage shape and textures, with flowering plants in bloom at different times.

---

trees & palms
Acacia podalyriifolia
Averrhoa carambola
Caesalpinia echinata
Caesalpinia peltophoroides
Cassia ferruginea
Citrus aurantium
Citrus limonia
Delonix regia
Eugenia uniflora
Jacaranda mimosaefolia
Livistona chinensis
Malvaviscus arboreus
Michelia champaca
Myrciaria cauliflora

Persea gratissima
Phoenix roebelenii
Pinus elliot
Syagrus romanzoffiana
Tabebuia impetiginosa
Tabebuia vellosoi
Tibouchina granulosa
Tibouchina mutabilis
shrubs & bamboos
Agave attenuata
Bambusa gracilis
Brunfelsia uniflora
Calliandra tweediei
Clerodendron fragans
Hydrangea macrophylla

Iresine herbstii
Punica granatum
Rhododendron simsii
groundcover
Agapanthus africanus
Axonopus compressus
Cymbidium x hybridum
Davallia fejeensis
Dendrobium primulinum
Dietes bicolor
Gusmania blassi
Heliconia collinsiana
Oncidium varicosum
Ophiopogum
    planiscapus 'Nigrescens'

Pentas lanceolata
Pilea microphylla
Solenostemon scutellarioides
Zoysia japonica
climbers & epiphytes
Bougainvillea glabra
x Laeliocattleya

Wisteria floribunda lightly clothes a pergola of white painted wood, creating a spectacular effect when it flowers at the same time as the *Rhododendron simsii*. Colour saturates both sky and ground as the petals drop.

03 the travellers' garden

orlando busarello | designer
location | curitiba

Imagine a place where it is possible to create harmony – or contrast – as desired, between European and tropical styles. A space where exotic flora is disciplined and where formality takes on a more relaxed feel, and the two spheres of the 'tropics' and the 'old world' graciously pay homage to one another. This extraordinary blend has been achieved by Orlando Busarello in the Travellers' Garden in Parana, in southern Brazil.

Located in the eastern part of the city of Curitiba, the property stands on an elevation with panoramic views of the coastal mountains and surrounding areas. Busarello decided to create a terraced garden that would both take advantage of the views and merge two cultures in one space.

In the form of a cube, the house has private areas located on the upper levels, where the surfaces are more closed, and living areas in the transparent lower level, with easy access to the garden and swimming pool. At the entrance, a white awning floats like a wing or sail over the lawn, extending the winter garden and forming a transitional space between interior and exterior.

The strict geometry of the building is carried into the garden, where pink granite is used for the hard landscaping. From the square swimming pool directly in front of the house, granite steps interplanted with grass invite guests to another level. This is occupied by a rectangular patio with a white wooden pergola at one end. Also based on a square, this three-dimensional structure is covered with *Wisteria floribunda*, creating a spectacular display as it blossoms in summer at the same time as the pink *Rhododendron simsii*. The thousands of petals that drop from these plants entirely cover the ground, making the patio the dazzling centrepiece of the season.

Conifers, including junipers and cypress, clipped to imitate Italy's grand gardens, provide tall sculptural elements. Dotted around the site, they are used both to create unexpected and arresting juxtapositions with tropical plants, such as bromeliads and agapanthus, and also to harmonize with vegetation from temperate climates, including *Magnolia* x *soulangeana* and *Iris germanica*. Highly unusual in Brazil, such planting combinations are made possible by Curitiba's unique climate, which has four well-defined seasons.

In Busarello's words this garden is 'a sanctuary that screens one from the urban chaos and stress of day-to-day life, it is a reflection of the real and imaginary journeys of the owners and their guests through fantastic worlds. It exalts the spirit and encourages the flight of fancy of curious and restless travellers.'

trees & palms

Araucaria angustifolia
  (Araucaria brasiliana)

Cedrus deodara

Chamaecyparis obtusa

Chamaecyparis pisifera

Cunninghamia lanceolata

Cupressus sempervirens

Eucalyptus cinerea

Lagerstroemia indica

Magnolia x soulangeana
  'Alba Superba'

Quercus rubra

Syagrus romanzoffiana

Tabebuia avellanedae

Thuja occidentalis

Tipuana tipu

shrubs & bamboos

Buxus sempervirens

Camellia japonica

Cycas revoluta

Gardenia jasminoides

Juniperus chinensis
  'Alba Variegata'

Juniperus communis

Juniperus virginiana

Phyllostachys pubescens

Rhododendron simsii

groundcover

Agapanthus africanus

Clivia miniata

Dendrobium nobile

Iris germanica

Ophiopogon japonicus

Paspalum notatum
  'Flugge'

climbers

Hedera helix

Plumbago capensis

Wisteria floribunda

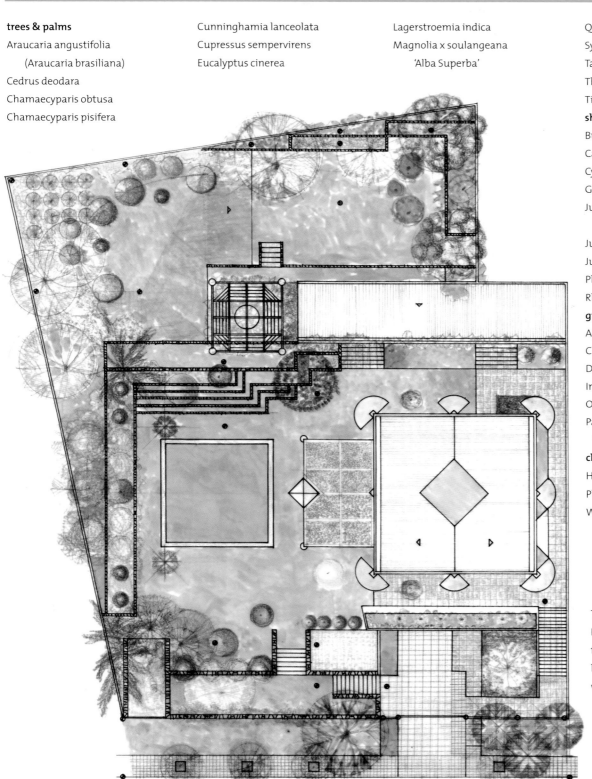

Tropics and old world merge in
Busarello's design – European
formality and exotic abundance
both seem to find a natural place
within the geometric layout.

left Cool whites, including agapanthus in containers, and greens are the dominant tones around the pergola – until the *Wisteria* and the rhododendrons burst into flower in spring.

above The magnificent blooms of *Magnolia* x *soulangeana* 'Alba Superba' bring a temperate feel to a tropical garden.

opposite Tall spires of *Cupressus sempervirens*, junipers and clipped conifers add another reference to European formality and restraint among the luxuriantly prolific tropical vegetation around the swimming pool.

Against the hazy blur of the distant skyline of São Paolo, the strong, clean shapes of Dantas' planting stand out sharply. Given ample space and in the context of such simplicity, Dantas used plants with giant leaves and exuberant flowers.

04 an ongoing project

anna maria prado dantas | designer
location | são paolo

Thirty years ago, Roberto Burle Marx worked on the design of this project in the Cidade Jardim district of São Paulo, an exclusive residential area near the government palace. The garden, which promised to be one of his many spectacular creations, was only partially completed, and the majority of his ideas were not implemented. As time passed, it was not properly maintained and the plants Burle Marx had specified were not thriving. Almost everything from the original concept vanished, apart from some mature trees.

Now the project has been revived, and it could not have been entrusted to a better professional than Anna Maria Prado Dantas. Like Burle Marx, she has a hands-on approach, creating and maintaining many of her gardens herself.

Most of the residence faces the rear garden, where the noise of the busy street beyond is barely audible. An additional advantage is the site's location on top of a hill, affording panoramic views through the glass façade of the house over the entire garden and beyond, to the high-rise buildings of the city in the hazy distance.

Dantas's design is clean and strong, encompassing an extensive central lawn, a swimming pool and a stone path crossing the garden. The clients – an artist and his family of seven children and numerous grandchildren – have to walk through the whole garden to reach a ceramics studio which the owner has built, along with an orchid house, where there was once a tennis court. Hard-landscaping

materials are unobtrusive, with Goias stones laid around the swimming pool and granite sets used elsewhere.

Against this restrained background Dantas's adventurous planting stands out as the main dramatic feature of the garden. Exploiting the advantages of ample space and excellent aspect, the majority of the plants are tropical, with giant leaves and exuberant flowers. One exception is *Rhododendron simsii*, found in abundance all over São Paulo. Unusual combinations of different textures and colours are found throughout the garden, with hues varying from the predominant yellow to red, plus coral orange and a touch of blue. Flowering plants are concentrated around the swimming pool, blossoming in spring and summer when they can be enjoyed. A single border of annuals, requested by the client, provides a sense of change.

Inventive and independent in her choice of plants, Dantas does not slavishly follow fashions and sometimes revives old varieties that have fallen out of favour. And because garden projects are a design process and not a product, she has the opportunity to continue introducing new plants. Recently she added trees to create more privacy for the clients as more houses are built all around.

Dantas continues her visits, advising on new plants and performing the specialized pruning, mulching and feeding that a garden needs all year round. In this way she combines her artistry and plant knowledge with the fundamental requirements of the garden.

trees & palms	shrubs	groundcover	climbers
Archontophoenix alexandrae	Acalypha reptans	Aloe arborescens	Jasminum polyanthum
Archontophoenix cunninghamii	Agave attenuata	Anthurium froebelii	Podranea ricasoliana
Dypsis decaryi	Allamanda puberula	Begonia coccinea	
Ficus elastica 'Decora'	Dracaena marginata	Dietes iridioides	
Salix babylonica	Ligustrum sinense	Hemerocallis flava	
Spathodea campanulata	Phormium tenax	Impatiens hybrida	
Tibouchina mutabilis	'Variegatum'	Ophiopogon japonicus	
Washingtonia filifera	Rhododendron simsii	Strelitzia reginae	
	Spiraea cantoniensis		

above Plants with bright flowers are used around the swimming pool, where clients and friends can relax on sunny days in the shade of palm trees. Splashes of different colours are added by *Allamanda puberula*, *Tibouchina mutabilis* and *Strelitzia reginae*.

right & opposite A simple but effective composition using natural boulders, flowering shrubs and groundcover plants, with statuesque trees towering overhead.

Dazzling in its complexity and
meticulously conceived, Duprat's
concept for the entire garden can be
appreciated in this bird's-eye view.
Patterns are continued across the
garden in a variety of hardscaping
materials and plants are treated as
important elements in the design.

05 bankboston headquarters

isabel duprat | designer
location | são paolo

An outstanding example of the successful integration of landscaping
and architecture, the BankBoston building in São Paulo's newest
financial district has one of the most celebrated contemporary public
gardens in the city. Serpentine paths, generous plazas and small
resting areas subdivide the space, covering almost 10,000 square
metres, all tied together by a strong, sinuous design. One aim of
landscape architect Isabel Duprat was to open up views in places and
then close them again in small resting areas, to stimulate a variety of
sensations and a feeling of the unpredictable.

Water flows through the garden, cascading down on one side of
the building to form a stream with colourful fish and aquatic plants,
and reappearing on the other as a darkly reflective sheet. In the heart
of the garden, in its most intimate space, is a pergola covered in plants
which filter the light falling on seats near the water.

Hard landscaping materials were chosen to echo those of the
building – predominantly glass and steel – but also according to
their function. Duprat stipulated small pebbles where a slow pace is
appropriate for meandering around the garden and in resting areas,
but where faster progress is required she used Portuguese mosaic.
Ochre-coloured mosaic in areas for cars and public access is
comfortable on the eye and reduces visual impact.

Duprat's adventurous and confident planting is in keeping with
the drama of the overall design. As if for the construction of a film
set, most of the trees were brought in as 10-metre tall specimens,
requiring well thought out structural supports and adequate soil,
since this is also a roof terrace. The specified plants were mostly
native Brazilian flora, both so that they could survive the harsh
city environment and add an educational aspect, as they include
indigenous plants that are either endangered or are no longer
common in planting palettes. Trees such as *Hymenaea courbaril*,
the rubber tree *Hevea brasiliensis*, *Cariniana legalis* and *Lecythis
pisonis* were treated as important elements in the garden.

The brazilwood, *Caesalpinia echinata*, which gave the country
its name – though ironically facing extinction – was celebrated by
being planted in groups on the central island in front of the building.
Syzygium malaccense, *Amherstia nobilis* and *Tabebuia avellanedae*
were selected for their spectacular flowers; while the jacaranda, in
addition to its gorgeous blooms, also provides a generous spread
of canopy. For architectural interest, Duprat used *Bombax ceiba*,
Erythrina crista-galli and the scented *Plumeria rubra* – frangipani.

Trees with different coloured or peeling bark, such as
Lagerstroemia indica and *Caesalpinia ferrea,* provide further
interest, as do fruit trees, which also attract large numbers of birds.
Shrubs, perennials, climbers and groundcover such as *Strelitzia
reginae*, *Jasminum nitidum* and *Gardenia jasminoides* create
a variety of volumes, textures and scents around the garden.
Grasses and sculptural plants are further elements in the profusion.

The garden is a magical space in an urban setting. For São Paulo,
it provides a fresh approach to city gardens, with beauty combined
with function, improving the quality of life for its inhabitants.

trees & palms

Amherstia nobilis
Balfourodendron
 riedelianum
Bombax ceiba
Caesalpinia echinata
Caesalpinia ferrea
Caesalpinia peltophoroides
Cariniana legalis
Cassia fistula
Cassia leptophylla
Clusia fluminensis
Cordia superba
Dypsis madagascariensis
Esenbeckia leiocarpa
Erythrina crista-galli
Erythrina mulungu
Eugenia brasiliensis
Eugenia involucrata
Eugenia uniflora
Hevea brasiliensis
Hymenaea courbaril
Jacaranda caroba
Lagerstroemia indica
Lagerstroemia speciosa
Lecythis pisonis
Lophanthera lactescens
Michelia champaca
Myrciaria cauliflora

Pachira aquatica
Peltophorum dubium
Plumeria rubra
Samanea saman
Schinus molle
Syagrus oleracea
Syzygium malaccense
Tabebuia avellanedae
Tabebuia chrysotricha
Tabebuia pentaphylla
Tibouchina mutabilis
Washingtonia filifera

shrubs & bamboos

Alpinia zerumbet
 'Variegata'
Bauhinia galpinii
Buxus sempervirens
Calliandra brevipes
Cycas revoluta
Dichorisandra thyrsiflora
Galphimia brasiliensis
Gardenia jasminoides
Hibiscus rosa-sinensis
Holmskioldia sanguinea
 'Citrina'
Ixora sp.
Ixora coccinea compacta
Jasminum mesnyi
Murraya exotica
Philodendron
 bipinnatifidum
Phyllostachys pubescens
Pogonatherum paniceum
Pontederia cordata
Punica granatum
Quisqualis indica
Rhododendron simsii
Thysanolaena maxima
Tibouchina mutabilis
Viburnum tinus
Zamia pumila

groundcover

Agapanthus africanus
Arachis repens
Arundina bambusifolia
Asparagus myriocladus
Barleria repens
Belamcanda chinensis
Callisia repens
Crinum procerum
Cryptanthus sp.
Dietes bicolor
Eragrostis curvula
Evolvulus pusillus
Gibasis schiedeana
Heliconia psittacorum
 'Sassy'
Heliconia psittacorum
Hemerocallis flava
Hemerocallis sp.
Hemigraphis sp.
Kalanchoe sp.
Lantana camara
Lysimachia congestiflora
Neomarica caerulea
Odontonema strictum
Ophiopogon jaburan
Ophiopogon jaburan
 'Variegata'
Ophiopogon japonicus
Pandanus baptistii
Pandanus racemosus
Pennisetum setaceum
 'Rubrum'
Pilea microphylla
Pilea nummulariifolia
Polygonum capitatum
Portulaca oleracea
Sansevieria cilindrica
Sansevieria trifasciata
 'Hahnii'
Schizocentron elegans

Spilanthes repens
Strelitzia juncea
Strelitzia reginae
Zoysia japonica

aquatics

Cyperus papyrus
Nymphaea alba
Typhonodorum
 lindleyanum

climbers

Bougainvillea spectabilis
Hedera helix
Hedera helix
 'Variegata'
Jasminum nitidum
Strongylodon macrobotrys

above left Profuse planting using trees, shrubs and climbers makes this public space a lush green oasis.

opposite Water flows through the garden and is utilized, along with every other available space, for riotous planting. The climber *Strongylodon macrobotrys* was trained over a wooden pergola, the natural timber of which contrasts well with the glass and stainless steel of the bank building – designed by Skidmore Owings & Merrill – though its structure and shape tie garden and architecture together.

above White-flowered azaleas were planted on one side of the snaking water course, while for contrast on the other is the exotic *Heliconia psittacorum*.

opposite above Groups of different plants with strong textures and character fill crevices and beds around the water feature, creating drama and interest. Some spaces offer seclusion and a sense of enclosure, while others open up views of the magnificent planting.

opposite below A great block of the startling bird-of-paradise flower *Strelitzia reginae* borders the driveway linking different parts of the garden. Ochre Portuguese mosaics mark pedestrian routes across the grey-paved vehicle access.

far left The patio built of salvaged stone is suffused with the pink-red petals dropped by the *Syzygium malaccense* tree.

left Duprat has skilfully tiered the planting up towards the Gávea Rock, bringing it into the garden.

below Surrounded by nature and mountains, the garden merges imperceptibly into the forest. A large expanse of lawn opens up views to the grandeur beyond.

06 alto da boa vista farm

isabel duprat | designer
location | rio de janeiro

It must feel like an enchantment to live in this romantic and idyllic place, encircled by the Tijuca forest and with the Gávea Rock – one of Rio de Janeiro's most celebrated landmarks – as part of the borrowed landscape. Great sensitivity was required to interact with this setting, respecting the natural beauty of the surroundings and bringing in the almost overwhelming landscape to realize some of the details, and then pulling back to acknowledge its monumental scale. Designer Isabel Duprat has ensured that the garden harmonizes with the natural tropical flora that surrounds the farm, but at the same time she has created an independent green space.

Duprat is a landscape architect who brings an attention to detail to whatever she designs. Having developed her skills in several research projects with botanists, she also had the opportunity to live and work with Roberto Burle Marx. In a career spanning 23 years, she has, as part of her philosophy, designed, installed and maintained gardens in one continuous creative process.

Here, a long drive winding through the garden leads to the house, from where the main elements of the garden are laid out to view, set dramatically against the background of the rugged mountains in the distance. For the swimming pool, placed at the furthest point from the house in a higher part of the property next to the forest, Duprat designed a deck of granite and *olho de sapo*, a Portuguese limestone.

Behind the house, a *Syzygium malaccense* tree forms the focal point of a large patio. Twice a year, in autumn and spring, it drops its bright pink-red petals, making a stunning carpet of colour. Its delicious red fruit evokes memories of childhood for anyone who has lived in a tropical country. In front of the patio, where the family spend most of their time, is a profusion of shrubs and colourful groundcover that enliven and enrich this area. An Italianate fountain in the middle of the large lawn adds the soothing sound of bubbling water.

The planting is uncompromisingly in the contemporary idiom, with large swathes of grasses, perennials and colourful foliage. Smaller perennials such as yellow daylily *Hemerocallis flava* and blue *Plumbago* enliven the composition and contrast with the untamed forest background. By planting palm trees and exotic plants such as *Caryota mitis*, *Heliconia rostrata* and strelitzia, and repeating them around the garden, Duprat created a rhythm, as well as bringing into the domestic space elements found in the natural environment. All the plants work together in the tropical light that gently bathes the foliage, intensifying the different green hues. 'In my designs I like to work with light and see the pattern formed in the areas of sun and shade and the nuances between them.'

Where there was formerly a tennis court, Duprat created a small pond crossed by stepping stones, which she planted with luxuriant aquatic plants; fish bring movement and life to the composition. As if all the space outside were not enough, there is also a winter garden inside the house. The lushness of the tropical vegetation, with its variegated and deep green foliage, brings natural freshness into the heart of the house.

trees & palms

Caesalpinia ferrea

Caesalpinia peltophoroides

Caryota mitis

Chrysalidocarpus lutescens

Dracaena arborea

Koelreuteria bipinnata

Phoenix roebelenii

Plumeria rubra

Ptychosperma macarthuri

Schizolobium parahyba

Syagrus romanzoffiana

Syzygium malaccense

Tabebuia avellanedae

Tibouchina mutabilis

shrubs

Cycas revoluta

Galphimia brasiliensis

Gardenia jasminoides

Grevillea banksii

Ixora coccinea compacta

Ixora undulata

Nerium oleander

Philodendron undulatum

groundcover

Alpinia purpurata

Arundina bambusifolia

Bulbine frutescens

Calathea zebrina

Canna x generalis

Crinum erubescens

Crinum procerum

Dietes iridioides

Evolvulus glomeratus

Heliconia psittacorum

Heliconia rostrata

Hemerocallis flava

Holmiskioldia sanguinea

Impatiens sp.

Ophiopogon japonicus

Pachystachys lutea

Pentas lanceolata

Philodendron williamsii

Phormium tenax

Peristrophe angustifolia

Schizocentron elegans

Spathiphyllum cannifolium

Spilanthes repens

Strelitzia augusta

Zoysia japonica

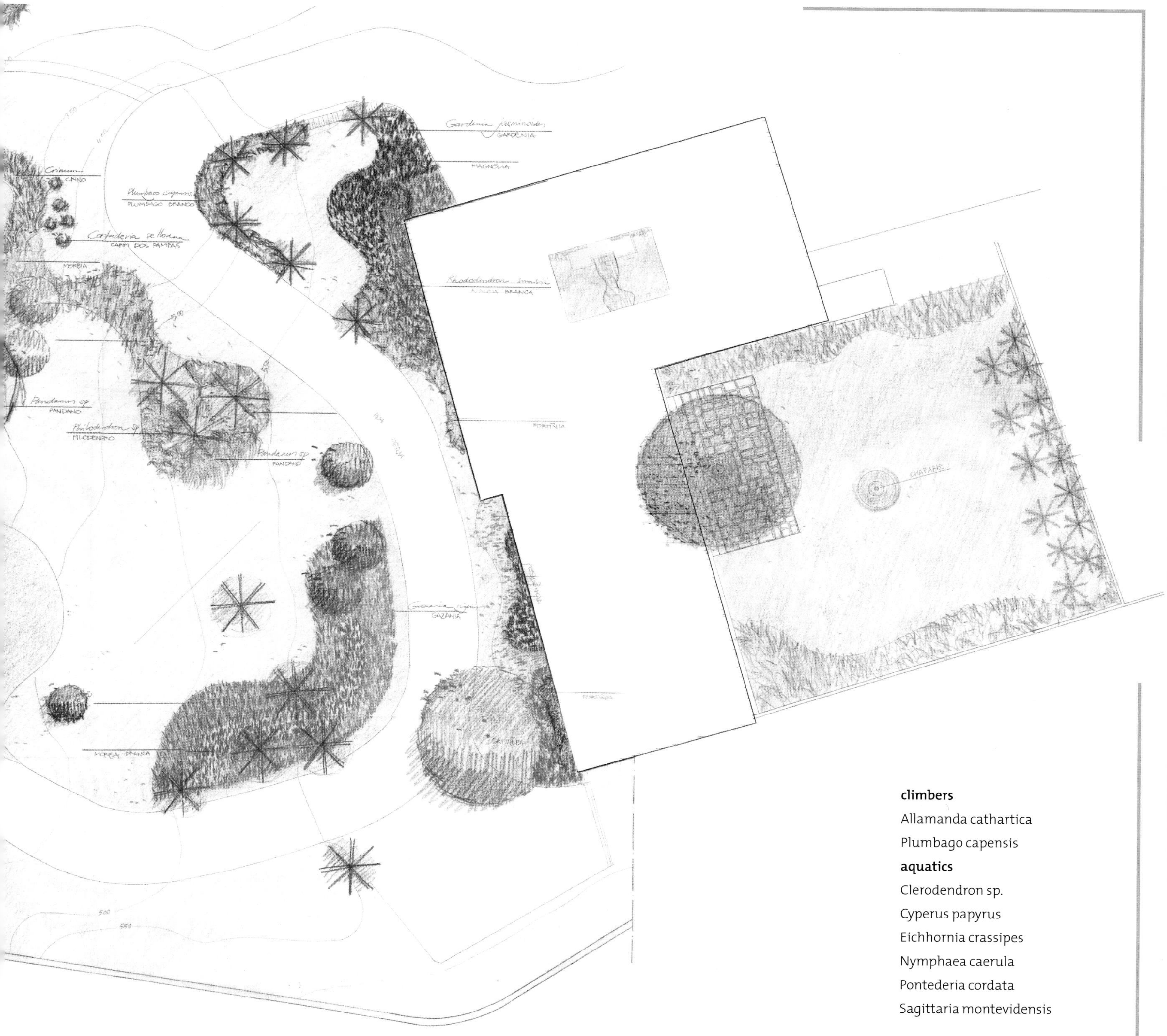

Crinum
CRINO

Plumbago capensis
PLUMBAGO BRANCO

Cortaderia selloana
CAPIM DOS PAMPAS

MOREIA

Pandanus sp
PANDANO

Philodendron sp
FILODENDRO

Pandanus sp
PANDANO

Gardenia jasminoides
GARDENIA

MAGNOLIA

Rhododendron boninse
AZALEIA BRANCA

FORTUNA

CHAFARIZ

Gazania rigens
GAZANIA

MOREIA BRANCA

FORTUNA

AZALEIA

climbers
Allamanda cathartica
Plumbago capensis
aquatics
Clerodendron sp.
Cyperus papyrus
Eichhornia crassipes
Nymphaea caerula
Pontederia cordata
Sagittaria montevidensis

right Designer Isabel Duprat has ensured that the planting in the garden echoes the natural tropical flora that surrounds the farm, but at the same time she has created a garden to be enjoyed by the owners.
below The sun gently bathes the grasses, irises and papyrus, making them glow in the light and enhancing the different textures and shades of green.

opposite Three views of the water feature, crossed by stepping stones and planted with luxuriant aquatic vegetation such as *Nymphaea* (water lilies) and *Cyperus papyrus* (papyrus). Around the margins are flowering shrubs and perennials which provide colour, reflected in the still surface of the water. Fish such as carp add movement and life to the composition.

Idyllically immersed in the forest, this new Brazilian country-style garden features architectural plants such as agaves and yuccas, together with colourful hydrangeas.

07 the three valleys

sonia infante | designer
location | petrópolis

Petrópolis is a small city near Rio de Janeiro, famous for the imperial palaces where the emperor Dom Pedro II had his favourite summer residence in the nineteenth century and now popular as a holiday and health resort. It was colonized by German settlers, who no doubt appreciated the temperate climate, which also suited the types of plants they were familiar with. The region has a mild climate during autumn and winter, while summer can be hot. These contrasts of warm and cool climate, the European influence and the tropical flora all contributed to the design of this country garden by Sonia Infante.

Close to the city but surrounded by mountains and the Atlantic forest, the garden at the São Judas Tadeo farm covers a huge area of 48,000 square metres. Three damp valleys already existed, with natural springs feeding myriad tiny streams. Infante was excited at the prospect of creating a garden on the grandest scale: 'I love working with large areas as I can express my creativity. Like Burle Marx, I think of gardening as painting on a large canvas with colours, texture and shapes in the form of plants.'

In a garden of this size, and in a setting of such magnificent scenery, Infante had to be expansive – the bigger the garden, the bolder and more generous the concept required. Infante achieved this by painting the land in large, colourful blocks of plants, as if it were an abstract composition. A major practical challenge was ensuring good drainage over such a large area, while avoiding creating problems in the future. New channels were dug, directing the water to an artificial lake, and timber bridges made of teak were constructed to cross them.

Once the canvas was prepared, the planting of the landscape composition could begin. Like Burle Marx, Infante grows her own plants on her farm nearby, which ensures that they are well adapted to the local climate and soil. She had free rein to design the garden and selected a large number of perennials, which have the advantage of flowering year after year, while shrubs and trees of different sizes give height and depth.

Large expanses of single species of perennials are interplanted with drifts of grasses, creating rhythms and modulations of light, colour and texture, like an orchestral score or a musical painting, changing in different parts of the garden and with the seasons. In spring the spikey bulbines and bold leaf shapes of zantedeschias contrast with the grassy foliage of moraeas; pink is provided by *Pentas lanceolata* and various ericas, and yellow by *Allamanda* and a riot of lilies. In summer blue is predominant, from agapanthus and hydrangeas, with splashes of yellow lilies and bright orange *Impatiens walleriana*. In autumn a striking combination of the white flowers of zantedeschias and lilac *Salvia mexicana* contrast with the orange of *Streptosolen* and the pink of *Tibouchina*. Even the long, cool winter months are brightened by the profusion of pink flowers of azaleas and rhododendrons, enhanced by the orange of lantanas.

Infante's inventive and original use of plants ensures that in each of these three interconnected magical valleys is a unique and secret garden.

With single species planted in great blocks, colours seems to flow through the garden, creating a composition on the grandest scale, as envisaged in a drawing for one of the valleys. In this view the yellow is provided by *Coreopsis lanceolata*, with the white flowers of *Zantedeschia aethiopica* in the centre. Hazy blues and purples come from *Agapanthus africanus* and *Salvia leucantha*. The surrounding forest provides a majestic backdrop for the garden and its colours.

shrubs	Chlorophytum comosum	Lilium candidum	Salvia leucantha
Hydrangea macrophylla	Coreopsis sp.	Moraea ramosa	Zantedeschia aethiopica
groundcover	Erica gracilis	Myosotis	**climbers**
Agapanthus africanus	Impatiens linearifolia	Pilea microphylla	Plumbago capensis
Ajuga reptans	Lantana camara	Pentas lanceolata	**aquatics**
Begonia semperflorens	Lavandula vera	Rhododendron simsii	Cyperus papyrus
Bulbine caulescens	Lespedeza	Russelia chamissoana	

opposite In this inventive planting composition Infante used hydrangeas, variegated yuccas, *Agave americana* and various groundcovers in a seamless carpet of colour and texture. Native cactuses were left as accent plants in true Brazilian style.

left Demonstrating a strong sense of colour, simple blocks of the orange-flowering *Impatiens walleriana* mark the ends of a rustic timber bridge across a stream.

below The architectural *Prunus campanulata* is underplanted with large abstract drifts of *Hydrangea macrophylla*, *Impatiens walleriana*, the white *Zantedeschia aethiopica* and *Dietes bicolor*. The painterly colours glow in the sunlight, in contrast to the dark shadows of the forest in the background.

far left Large areas of single species' planting are a trademark of Orsini's work. Tall *Phoenix dactylifera* emerge from a foam of groundcover and echo the structure of a pavilion.
left Looking out into the landscape from the museum's veranda the eye is drawn from the vrieseas in the foreground to the mass of tropical trees forming a backdrop.
below A path made of large Ouro Preto quartzite slabs leads visitors around the verdant landscape.

08 a tropical paradise

luiz carlos orsini | designer
location | minas gerais

Minas Gerais, in the southeast of Brazil, is very different from the usual, flamboyant stereotype of the country. Enclosed by mountains, its well-preserved baroque colonial villages are filled with art, whether in shops selling antiques and crafts, or in the picturesque streets and hundreds of churches. The climate is amiable, the landscape breathtaking and even the food tastes different. Sometimes it can seem like time stands still here. However, the more adventurous explorer will come across the unexpected and the sublime. As a cultural oasis, the Contemporary Art Centre Inhotim (CACI), is one of those places that takes the breath away – a combination of museum and park, it is a space where modern art and architecture and landscape design come together in a way that rarely happens.

In 1993, landscape designer Luiz Carlos Orsini was commissioned to develop a project in this extensive former farm, initially restoring an area designed by Roberto Burle Marx and Pedro Nehring César. It was only in 1999, when the idea of developing the art centre emerged, that Orsini began working on other areas. Four large lakes were created, one of which provides the setting for an art installation called 'True Rouge' by the Brazilian artist Tunga.

To accommodate the client's important art collection, the architect Paulo Orsini designed a pavilion and seven other buildings placed strategically around the property. Luiz Orsini's landscape project has a significance equal to the architecture in the development of the arts centre, not only as a way of attracting visitors, but also for its intrinsic botanical interest and dramatic planting compositions. 'This project has a fundamental role in the ecological balance of the area, considering the diversity of the vegetation that enriches the environment, creating a local ecosystem that attracts wild animals and local birds from the region', Orsini explains.

Hundreds of specimens of the tree *Beaucarnea recurvata*, with its curious pyramidal trunk and tufts of leaves, were used along the paths and in blocks, in theatrical, almost surreal displays. Broad sweeps of species were planted, providing volume and texture, including the bromeliad *Vriesea regina*, spikey *Agave wercklei* and *Duranta repens* with its lilac flowers and golden yellow berries. The yellow and red splashed foliage of *Codiaeum variegatum* and orange and blue flowers of *Strelitzia juncea* inject more colour, while for accents in the borders Orsini introduced the large-scale fronds and fans of *Cycas revoluta*, *Chamaerops humilis* and *Caryota mitis*.

The garden is a tropical paradise where sculptures are placed in ideal settings, giving the impression that they have spontaneously arisen there, and where the intrinsic beauty of the plants and the sheer magnitude of the place provide visitors with a constant source of wonder.

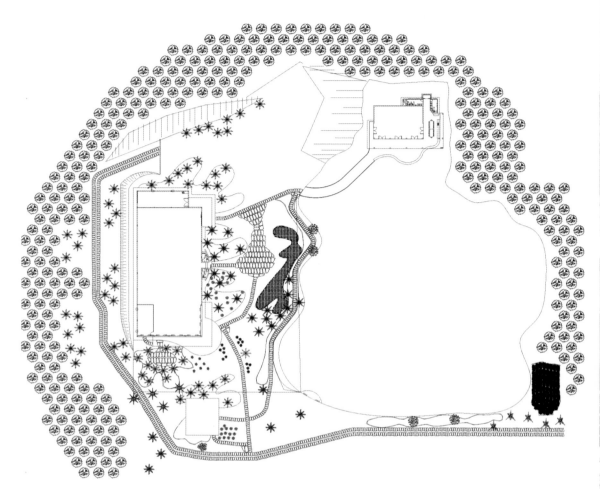

trees & palms	Myrciaria cauliflora	Cycas revoluta	Strelitzia juncea
Arecastrum romanzoffianum	Neodypsis decaryi	Murraya paniculata	Tulbaghia violacea
Areca triandra	Phoenix canariensis	**groundcover**	Vriesea fosteriana
Beaucarnea recurvata	Phoenix dactylifera	Aechmea 'Electrica'	Vriesea reginae
Bismarckia nobilis	Phoenix roebelenii	Agave wercklei	Zoysia japonica
Caryota urens	Phoenix rupicola	Chlorophytum comosum	**climbers & epiphytes**
Chamaedorea erumpens	Pinanga kuhli	Clivia miniata	Neoregelia sp.
Chamaerops humilis	Ptychosperma elegans	Codiaeum variegatum	Syngonium podophyllum
Chrysalidocarpus lucubensis	Rhapis excelsa	Duranta repens 'Aurea'	
Chrysalidocarpus lutescens	Roystonea oleracea	Liriope platyphylla 'Variegata'	
Corypha elata	Wodyetia bifurcata	Neoreglia 'Fireball'	
Cyrtostachys lakka	**shrubs & bamboos**	Ophiopogon japonicum	
Dypsis leptocheilos	Bambusa gracilis	Philodendron bipinnatifidum	
Licuala grandis	Cycas circinalis	Philodendron sp.	

below & opposite above Orsini's use of repeated specimens of the palm *Beaucarnea recurvata* creates an almost surreal, otherworldly landscape.

opposite below Palm trees rise from a green bank sloping into one of the project's lakes, creating abstract forms using the landscape itself and a restrained palette of planting.

above left One of the buildings is approached by a curving concrete bridge; architecture and garden are towered over, but not overpowered by, the great bank of trees behind.

above centre & right Seating becomes sculpture in these timber benches made in Trancoso, Bahia. Cactuses, bromeliads and palms add their naturally sculptural shapes.

left To give height, Orsini planted tall palm trees rising sheer out of the ground, underplanting them sparsely with *Agave wercklei*. An art installation by the Brazilian artist Tunga fits in completely naturally with the planting scheme.

opposite Four large lakes were created in this ambitious landscape project, forming sublime settings for artworks, vegetation and architecture. Planting around them continues themes found elsewhere in Orsini's design – strong verticals provided by clean, uncluttered trunks of trees, with blocks and strips of massed planting beneath.

The giant and stately trunks of the royal palm tree *Roystonea oleracea* line the steps to the house like huge columns. Clipped balls of box add a touch of formality, lightened by summer-flowering bright pink *Mussaenda erythrophylla* 'Queen Sirikit'.

09 colouring the landscape

marcelo novaes | designer
location | campinas

The classic American lines of the house inspired this colourful and confident garden designed by Marcelo Novaes. Set in the country near Campinas, São Paulo, it takes advantage of a beautiful valley and a natural, steep, south-facing slope. Working with the topography of the site, a major aim of Novaes was to integrate the existing views into the lines of the garden.

The slope was the most challenging part of the project, dropping twenty meters from the level of the house to the bottom of the valley. Instead of steps, Novaes designed ramps to hug the contours of the land, allowing the slope to fall away naturally so that people can walk up or down comfortably and children can run and play safely.

Positioned on a level section in front of the house, the swimming pool enjoys views over the valley, and adjacent to it Novaes placed a kiosk where food and drinks can be served when entertaining. Further away, in the most secluded part of the garden, is a gazebo to provide shade on sunny days. This is a place to sit and relax, soothed by the sound of water from a concrete water feature attached to the scorching orange wall.

Novaes used a limited selection of hardscaping materials, both to provide unity in the design and to keep it simple. At the entrance, rustic granite blocks form the steps up to the house; to surround the swimming pool he selected Goias stone, a traditional material; and for the path he specified elegant Portuguese mosaic.

Passionate about plants, the client wanted the spectacular vegetation to be the central focus of the garden and worked closely with the designer on the schemes for this extensive property, covering 4,000 square metres. Tall and stately *Roystonea oleracea* palms tower over clipped *Buxus sempervirens* at the side of the steps leading to the entrance of the house, while a row of pink *Mussaenda erythrophylla* 'Queen Sirikit' was planted for its colour. Novaes also used *Tibouchina mutabilis* 'Nana' to greet visitors in wintertime.

A variety of palm trees were used around the property, and perhaps the key-note plant for the whole project is the extraordinary *Bismarckia nobilis*, originally from Madagascar, with its great fans of leaves. The pale bluish hues of its foliage contrast well with the green of the lawn.

Exotic bromeliads, mainly in yellows and reds, form dazzling blocks of colour against the blue tiles of the swimming pool. Towards the pergola are several examples of the Australian foxtail palm *Wodyetia bificarta*, underplanted with feathery *Asparagus myersii* and *Lysimachia congestiflora*.

At the end of a path, where another breathtaking view overlooks the valley, a rampant jade vine, *Strongylodon macrobotrys*, clambers over the wooden pergola, displaying its extraordinary flowers and releasing its scent over the garden. In this area for rest and contemplation Novaes calmed down the colours, specifying just a few species of palm and heliconias to avoid competing with the beauty of the landscape beyond.

trees & palms

Hyophorbe lagenicaulis

Pandanus utilis

Phoenix rupicola

Roystonea oleracea

Senna polyphylla

Tibouchina mutabilis 'Nana'

Wodyetia bifurcata

shrubs & bamboos

Acalypha reptans

Buxus sempervirens

Cycas revoluta

Impatiens hawkeri

Ixora coccinea compacta

Ixora macrothyrsa

Mussaenda alicia

Mussaenda erythrophylla
'Queen Sirikit'

Phyllostachys pubescens

Pleomele reflexa 'Variegata'

Ravenala madagascariensis

groundcover

Aechmea blanchetiana

Alcantarea imperialis

Alpinia zerumbet
'Variegata'

Asparagus myersii

Begonia cucullata

Cuphea gracilis

Heliconia rostrata

Lysimachia congestiflora

Zoysia japonica

climbers & epiphytes

Neoregelia 'Fireball'

Strongylodon macrobotrys

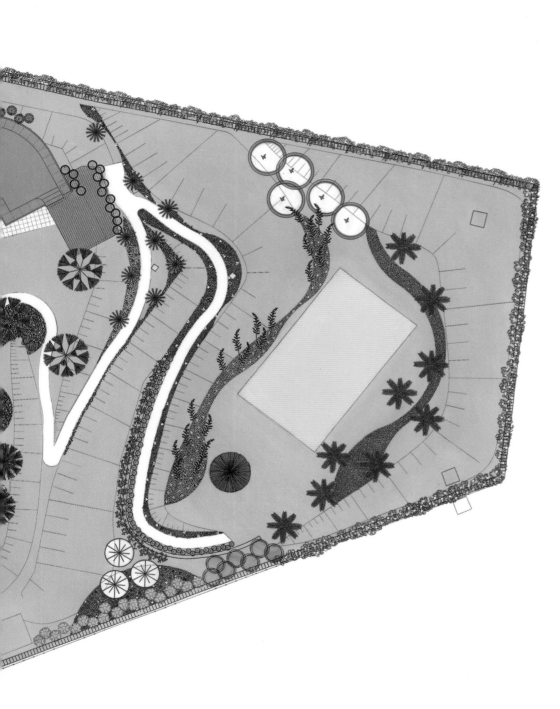

above Steps leading from a veranda are surrounded with blocks of different foliage shapes and colours, including the exotic *Asparagus myersii*. Novaes also used multiple specimens of the curious *Hyophorbe lagenicaulis* – the aptly named bottle palm.
below Strong hues are provided by both hard and soft landscaping – the deep blue tiles lining the swimming pool, the rustic timber of the diagonal decking, green fans of palm fronds, and the hot reds and yellows of bromeliads – creating a dynamic fusion of colours, forms and textures.

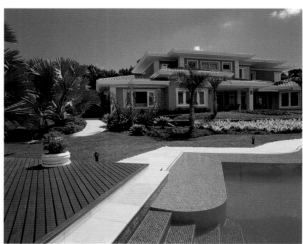

left A path of Portuguese mosaic slices across the steep grassy slope, combining practical function with dramatic effect. Further contrast is provided by the juxtaposition of the natural, untamed vegetation of the valley and the man-made landscape, planted with the spiky palm *Bismarckia nobilis* and the vivid colour of massed *Impatiens walleriana*.

right, above & centre Two views of a pergola covered by the climber *Strongylodon macrobotrys* demonstrate the opulent planting in this garden. Palm trees *Hyophorbe lagenicaulis* and *Wodyetia bifurcata* add height, while flowering plants and shrubs give colour – especially *Impatiens walleriana* planted en masse in an ecstatic composition.

right below A detail of the entrance to the residence, where Novaes designed the drive and steps in gentle curving lines made from natural granite. The palm *Roystonea oleracea* soars above, while closer to eye level are *Pleomele reflexa*, *Ixora coccinea compacta*, *Buxus sempervirens* and *Lysimachia congestiflora*.

abstraction

abstraction

Of all the arts, abstract painting is the most difficult. It demands that you know how to draw well, that you have heightened sensitivity for composition and for colours, and that you be a true poet. This last is essential.

Wassily Kandinsky

Landscape and garden design, like architecture, have always been influenced by art. Abstraction – a form of artistic activity that extracts an idea and transforms it into something that is not an accurate, true representation of reality – finds a perfect expression in the Brazilian landscape. In fact, one of the aspects that distinguishes Brazilian landscape design from the rest of the tropical world is its renowned use of abstraction.

More precisely, abstract expressionism, as distinct from two other major forms of abstraction – cubism and neoplasticism – is the term that perhaps best defines the main language of landscape in this

previous pages Hot & Cold (p. 135).
left A striking entrance to a country residence in São Paulo displays a precise linearity. The verticals of the slatted timber fence are picked up by the rows of palm trees along the undeviating straight path. Diagonal lines in the paving are continued into the garden surface.
opposite above Gleba Park is one of the most celebrated projects designed by Fernando Chacel in Rio de Janeiro. His ecological approach to planting design uses native plants combined with fluid and abstract lines.

country. Incorporating ideas borrowed from Surrealism and inspired by a desire to liberate art from tradition, abstract expressionism has a more fluid design, as seen in the work of Wassily Kandinsky or Jackson Pollock, or indeed in the free concept of nature itself.

In Brazilian landscape design, its major exponent is undoubtedly Roberto Burle Marx. He achieved complete spontaneity in shapes and forms, with primary colours and bold designs achieved sometimes with living material – blocks of single species of plants – and at other times with stones and natural elements.

This form of artistic expression is in complete contrast to the picturesque tradition of landscapes found in America and Europe in the nineteenth century. In a temperate climate the shapes and textures of the natural flora – and even the light – tend to be soft, gentle and intimate, creating a romantic atmosphere. In Brazil, on the other hand, the exuberant flora, untamed tropical jungles and strong, brilliant light create a more extrovert and chaotic atmosphere, evoking a spirit of adventure and fantasy, and a sense of journeying into the unconscious.

Of course, examples of abstract design can be found in gardens in other chapters, such as Jamil Jose Kfouri's dazzling swimming pool and the expansive, abstract shapes of Sonia Infante's planting in the three valleys. It is a form of design that permeates gardens and landscapes throughout Brazil, but the examples of projects included here are chosen to demonstrate the complex theoretical and artistic layers that create an abstract garden.

In this chapter, the intriguing ideas behind this form of art can be discerned, for instance, in the Mondrian-grid configuration of the

Lutchenberg garden by Orlando Busarello. And to find a perfect and deceptively simple form of abstraction you can travel to the garden of a former café farm designed by Ana Maria Bovério. In a stunning residential garden you can puzzle over how Luiz Carlos Orsini successfully mixed the formality of a grid shape with a more fluid design, and in Gilberto Elkis's rectangular red swimming pool, reminiscent of Mark Rothko, it is possible to experience the contrasting sensations of hot and cold. Abstraction can be achieved in both hard and soft landscaping, as demonstrated by Suely Suchodolsky and Elza Niero in the Daccache garden. Finally, rest your senses in the green of a spacious and elegant garden designed by Luciano Fiaschi.

far left A low, organically shaped retaining wall travels around this garden designed by Suely Suchodolsky and Elza Niero, extending in a continuous curve around a tree and creating islands for perennial planting. The curvilinear, natural forms meet a sharp contrast in the rectilinear chevrons of the decking.
left Abstraction prevails in this simple but clever device – repeated wooden box planters containing *Sansevieria trifasciata* lined up against a monochromatic white wall.

far left Making the transition between public and private space, a red sandstone raised bed contains the bright blue *Plumbago capensis*.
left Sharply defined walls and access steps in red sandstone are softened by billowing bougainvillea. The exotic blooms and exhilarating perfume of *Gardenia jasminoides* add further sensual stimuli.
below The clean verticals of palm trees rise from a rational and geometrical chequerboard pattern, with squares filled with different coloured plants and pebbles.

01 grillo lutchenberg garden

orlando busarello | designer
location | curitiba

Demonstrating what can be achieved in a restricted space, Orlando Busarello installed this attractive small garden, covering an area of just 400 square metres, around a house in a residential district in Curitiba, Parana. In a design based on interlocking geometrical shapes, Busarello skilfully accommodated a pergola, a kitchen garden, a belvedere, a terrace and a pool; the result is a contemporary and original space, diverse in functions and rich in interest for the users.

In a well-balanced combination of conceptual and practical applications, the garden can be regarded as a project of architectonic interventions, built on a solid theoretical foundation. The house was simply introduced on the long, narrow site with minimum impact on the natural and built environment. Busarello established a connection between the various available spaces, designing a garden that could be viewed as a piece of art but also completely inhabited by the clients. A second major achievement was the creation of an urban retreat – providing peace, relaxation, calm and a social setting for the occupants, in a time and place where these are rare and sought-after qualities.

At the entrance visitors are greeted by the climber *Bougainvillea spectabilis* trained as a small tree over a metallic support. When in bloom, its electric pink flowers transform a simple idea into a dramatic focal point. Several raised beds built of red Parana sandstone line the entrance and contain *Plumbago capensis, Dietes bicolor*, red-flowered *Rhododendron thomsonii* and erect evergreen *Cupressus sempervirens* planted in blocks and lines to create clear, definite shapes.

On one side of the house where there is no access to the garden the designer filled the space with a chequerboard pattern on a strict grid. Divided by lines of granite, the squares formed are filled with gravel and pebbles of different textures and colours. Single specimens of the bamboo *Phyllostachys pubescens* were planted in each square, the whole forming an abstract composition that can be appreciated from inside the house through the glass windows.

The chequerboard motif is repeated throughout the garden, at perpendicular and oblique angles to the house and in repeated modules of different materials. Slatted wooden decking was laid in the same units; and, taking the grid into the third dimension, a pergola was constructed with white structural members and cylindrical supporting pillars which echo the strong vertical elements of bamboos and palms used elsewhere in the garden. Softening the hard lines, a *Wisteria floribunda* trained over the pergola cascades down freely, providing shade beneath. A small rectangular lawn culminates the rational plan of this garden – an intriguing blend of disciplined forms, textures and structure, interwoven with flowers, grass and pebbles.

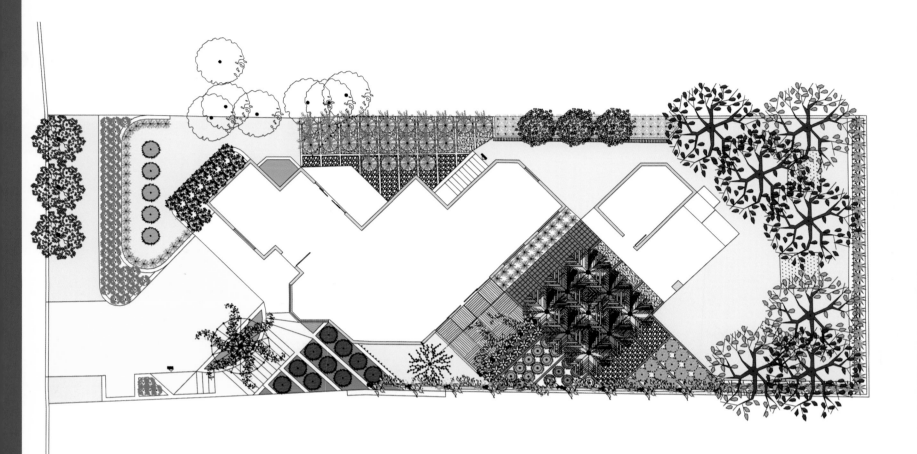

trees & palms

Acer palmatum 'Dissectum'

Cupressus sempervirens

Juniperus chinensis

Lagerstroemia indica

Myrciaria trunciflora

Syagrus romanzoffiana

Tibouchina mutabilis

shrubs & bamboos

Gardenia jasminoides

Hydrangea macrophylla

Phyllostachys pubescens

Rhododendron simsii

Rhododendron thomsonii

groundcover

Agapanthus africanus

Anthurium x froebelli

Axonopus compressus

Dietes bicolor

Dietes iridioides

Spathiphyllum wallisii

climbers

Boungainvillea spectabilis

Plumbago capensis

Wisteria floribunda

A playful but disciplined use of geometry runs throughout the garden. Square modules are repeated in different sizes and materials, and planting also plays its part in this rational, abstract design. Wooden decking, transparent roofing and pergola achieve a successful integration of interior and exterior spaces.

right A shady, potentially rather gloomy corner of the garden is lit up by the glowing canes and airy foliage of *Phyllostachys pubescens* planted on a strict orientation. The underlying grid is composed of lines of granite filled with different coloured gravels and pebbles.

In a clean modern design, Bovério uses the geometry of spheres, circles, rectangles and squares – and the interactions between them – in a classically abstract composition.

02 largo do café

ana maria bovério | designer
location | campinas

A surprise awaits visitors to the Largo do Café garden in Campinas, near São Paulo, as they pass through a traditional old farm house to discover a compelling modernist garden. Ana Maria Bovério designed this clean and minimalist space as part of an installation in a public park, and had to face the challenge of creating a project that would succeed in two distinct phases. Its first manifestation was as a garden installed as part of an architectural and landscape exhibition; the second incarnation was far more exciting, as the space was donated to the public and is now used by a diverse range of people.

A strong abstract and contemporary feel underpins the garden, which covers 1,155 square metres. Bovério has drawn upon a variety influences and references, including the American school of Eckbo, Halprin and Peter Walker, as well as the Mexicans Luis Barragán and Ricardo Legorreta. And the legacy of Burle Marx can be traced in the use of native tropical flora and the elegant lines in the shapes of borders and surfaces.

In her choice of hardscaping materials the designer specified only those appropriate for public spaces – ones that are durable, quick to install and easy to maintain. In addition she took into consideration aspects of sustainability and a regard for the environment. Colours are on the whole cool and neutral.

Well-defined lines and axes in relation to the building mark out and divide the space. Each of the elements, including the water feature, the sculptural walls pierced with slits, timber decks and the striking large spheres have an assertive presence, but combine in a well-balanced and integrated composition. Informal and curving lines break the orthogonality that prevails in the general layout, including the beautifully sculptured walls and the decking, long and shallow, that gently lead towards the building designed by the architects Jannini & Sagarra.

Bovério used plants with good texture and sculptural shapes, such as *Cycas revoluta*, phormiums, agaves, phoenix palms and yuccas, planted in raised rectangular beds. Beyond one boundary specimens of the tree *Caesalpinia peltophoroides* encircle the area, providing a more free-form background for the geometric shapes within the enclosure of the garden space. Colourful groundcover plants add dynamism.

Water is a constant element in Bovério's work. Her original idea here was for a pool of calm, reflecting water with a path of precast concrete paving allowing visitors to circulate, sit and get close to the water. To add interest as well as movement and sound, she then inserted a rectangular block fountain in the centre of the pool.

As early evening settles over the garden, subtle lighting effects consisting of twenty fibre-optic lights set into the pool create a wholly new experience of the garden. Then, suddenly, we may be startled as a colourful local tropical toucan lands on a nearby branch, as if it were the natural spirit of the place.

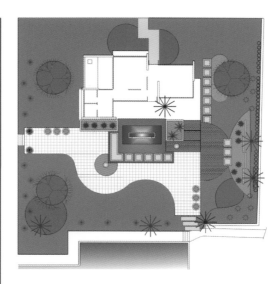

trees & palms

Beaucarnea recurvata

Bismarckia nobilis

Chamaerops humilis

Phoenix roebelenii

Pinanga coronata

shrubs & groundcover

Agave angustifolia

Agave sisalana

Cycas revoluta

Phormium tenax

Sansevieria trifasciata

Yucca elephantipes

Yucca filamentosa

A precise s-curve marks the boundary between paving and planted surface. Architectural plants such as agaves, phormiums and palms add their wildly sculptural shapes to the more abstract, geometric elements of the design.

In the evening, the architecture, timber decking, water feature and plants are all transformed by special lighting effects.

opposite above left Yuccas, agaves and *Cycas revoluta* were used as accent plants, among low groundcover planted in blocks of various colours and shapes.

opposite above right & below The water feature is a place where visitors can simply rest and contemplate, or circulate using the concrete stepping stones.

above & right As the sun sets, lighting adds another dimension to the garden, revealing new details and hidden perspectives. The long slits in the white wall offer intriguing glimpses beyond, while phormiums in containers look even more dramatic than by day.

Changes of level create a steep slope along one boundary, planted with a line of extraordinary *Yucca gloriosa*. A simple stepping stone path edged with rhododendrons leads up to the house – views beyond are glimpsed through the dissected architecture.

03 formality x abstraction

luiz carlos orsini | designer

location | belo horizonte

'To reinvent and divide a space and learn how to appreciate and enhance natural aspects in the landscape, to re-dimension it according to an aesthetic thought, demands knowledge and imagination. Nevertheless, there is another very important element: emotion – the emotion of creating something new and unique.' From these verbal fragments we can discern how garden designer Luiz Carlos Orsini sets about developing ideas for his commissions that take him all over Brazil.

In this particular project, built in Pampulha, a beautiful district of modern architecture in Belo Horizonte, Minas Gerais, Orsini designed a stylish garden based on a strong grid-inspired geometry. With this firm foundation, he was then able to liberate parts of the garden, creating contrasting, freer and more abstract shapes. Covering a total area of 7,800 square meters, the property provided sufficient space in which to develop this unusual but striking design.

Fortunately for Orsini, the landscape project was begun at the same time as the construction of the house, enabling him to synchronize his ideas and requirements with the other professionals involved – an ideal situation for any garden designer. But before construction could begin, level areas had to be imposed on the existing uneven natural terrain to accommodate the house. Orsini designed elegant steps up to the building and a series of sculptural landforms consisting of banks and retaining walls to hold the soil and vegetation in place. A long Cor-Ten steel wall, rising a few inches from the ground and creating ridges on the land, is an original use of this material.

Orsini's design respects the straight lines of the architecture of Luiz Antonio Lanza, in a minimal and harmonious style backed up with a restrained, structural use of mature plants and vegetation. Some existing native trees, such as jackfruit and cedar, were retained close to the building, and to enhance rather than compete with the cool simplicity of the surroundings Orsini simply introduced shrubs and tall trees, as well as gravel and a large lawn.

In summing up his feelings about this project he concludes that 'the emotion is translated here in the choice and distribution of the vegetation, colours, shapes and textures and the whole concept of manipulating the landform.'

above At the main entrance to the house, Orsini designed elegant steps made from unpolished granite and quartzite cobbles. On one side only he planted the exquisite *Sansevieria cylindrica*. Spreading a canopy over everything is the sculptural form of an already existing cedar.

right In this unusual composition of abstract shapes and minimalist planting, Orsini created different levels by introducing retaining edges made of Cor-Ten steel. He then planted a large drift of the silver-leaved *Sansevieria grandis*, as well as *Euphorbia xylophylloides*, *Acrocomia aculeata* and *Pedilanthus tithymaloides*.

trees & palms
Acrocomia aculeata
Caesalpinia ferrea
Ficus benjamina
Melaleuca leucadendron
Myrciaria cauliflora
Phoenix dactylifera
Plumeria alba

shrubs
Azalea sp.
Buxus semperflorens

Dracaena marginata
Eugenia sprengelii
Myrtus sp.
Viburnum tinus
Yucca sp.

groundcover
Arachis repens
Clivia miniata
Dietes bicolor
Dietes iridioides
Duranta repens 'Aurea'

Euphorbia xylophylloides
Iris sp.
Orchids
Pedilanthus tithymaloides
Sansevieria cylindrica
Sansevieria grandis
Schinus terebinthifolius

climbers
Hedera canariensis

top, left to right Contrasts between formal and abstract design are visible in various views of the house and garden. Along a long retaining wall on the left side of the house, an evenly spaced line of mature *Acrocomia aculeata* palm trees was installed, underplanted with *Dietes iridioides*. At the back of the house the formal geometry of the grid framework is more apparent, where a series of large gravel squares contain single specimens of the architectural Phoenix palm. Another angle shows the clean and well-defined edges of Orsini's design, respecting the modern minimalist architecture of the house. Orsini kept the planting restrained, using abstract shapes of single species planting, including *Sansevieria* sp.

above left A more enclosed part of the garden lies in front of the private rooms of the house. Elements of Japanese garden style were incorporated, including natural rocks, gravel and rhododendrons.

above right A series of steps in the form of small platforms leads visitors up to the front of the house.

Suchodolsky used the material Fulget – white pebbles set in concrete – like liquid paint, in order to create fluid forms in the ground surface.

04 daccache

suely suchodolsky & elza niero | designers
location | ibíuna

In a prime example of abstraction, Suely Suchodolsky and Elza Niero transformed what was once an empty and lifeless area into a tranquil and poetic garden in the city of Ibiúna. But first, the entire area of this large garden of 8,800 square metres had to be raised by a height of ten metres to accommodate the best views – a massive undertaking that would be prohibitively expensive in many countries.

From the inception of the project, the landscape designers had the full collaboration of both the architect of the house, Arnaldo Martino, and the clients. The best gardens are often a result of such sympathetic interactions. It was also fortunate that the owners had a sensibility for plants, art, architecture and design, and were distinguished art collectors.

'We studied the architecture and took into consideration the visual and environmental aspects of the surroundings and the clients' brief,' says Niero. Part of this brief was to find a space in the garden for the clients' sculptures, as well as to create an orchard around the house. Other elements requested were a tennis court, a swimming pool, a walk, a large lawn and 'an area where the children could feel they were in a place full of fantasy and imagination, a jungle-like doll's house'.

Long meandering paths wind around the garden and lead to these various elements, passing between curving walls made of bricks from the client's own former ceramics factory. One of the unique features created specifically for this project was the 'amoeba garden'. Like an abstract expressionist painting, the lines of the paving loosen and become more fluid and informal, in configurations that Suchodolsky designed on site. The material used here was Fulget – Italian washed white pebbles set in coloured concrete that is then polished – which Suchodolsky used like paint. Inspiration for the shapes came from the flowing forms found in nature, in contrast to the man-made, rigid lines of the architecture of the modern house. Other hardscaping in the garden consists of Portuguese mosaic, pebbles and specially designed brick.

In displaying the clients' sculptures, the designers positioned each one in a site-specific exercise. The artworks stand out strongly against the other elements in the landscape and, to avoid distracting attention away from them, vegetation was used here more as a background material. In open spaces individual specimens or small groups of plants are purposefully placed, acting as a kind of punctuation. The desired orchard was planted near the house and around the perimeter – as well as dividing the space and screening views of the recreational areas, it transforms the garden into a leafy and green urban retreat.

right Paths snaking around the garden are mostly made from Fulget and white Portuguese mosaic. In the centre, and positioned precisely, a piece of sculpture by the artist Megume is framed by simple blocks of vegetation, with the majestic mountain scenery forming a backdrop.

below right An informal and fluid transition was achieved between the private area of the garden and recreational ones. The sculpture, again by Megume, is counterpointed by a circle of plants.

left Architectural plants form punctuation points around the clean lines of the swimming pool area. Portuguese mosaic was used for the paving around the pool.

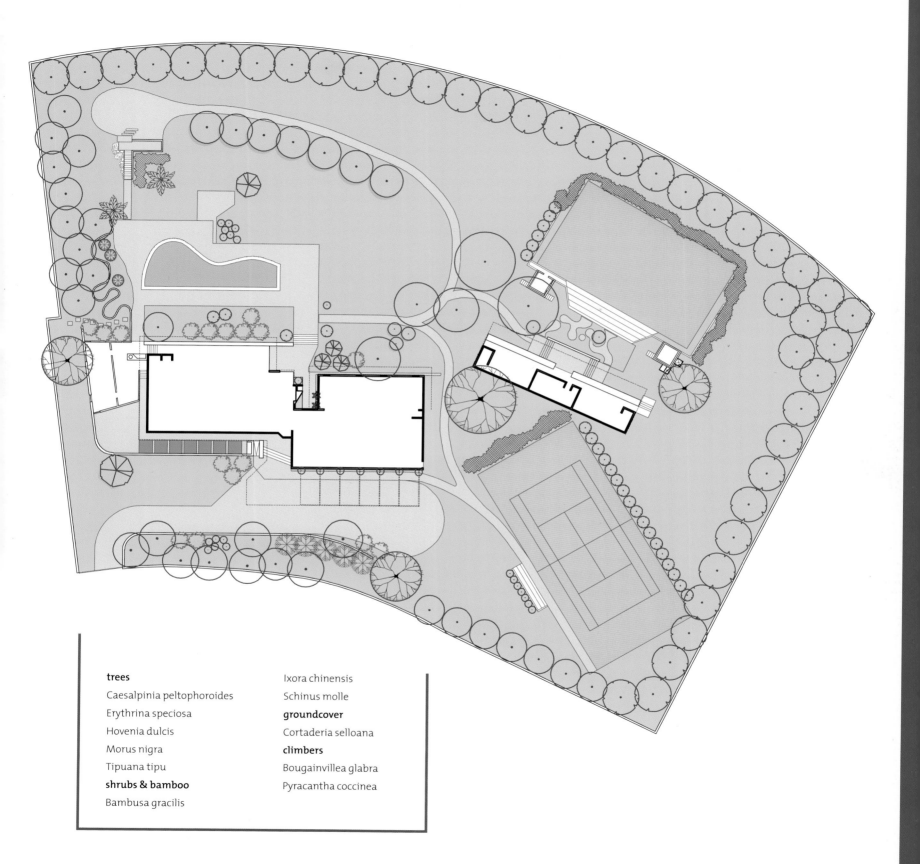

trees

Caesalpinia peltophoroides

Erythrina speciosa

Hovenia dulcis

Morus nigra

Tipuana tipu

shrubs & bamboo

Bambusa gracilis

Ixora chinensis

Schinus molle

groundcover

Cortaderia selloana

climbers

Bougainvillea glabra

Pyracantha coccinea

The blood-red swimming pool creates an almost bizarre contrast with the São Paulo skyline in the distance.

05 hot & cold

gilberto elkis | designer

location | são paolo

A striking red stripe of a swimming pool across the skyline is surely one of the most dramatic gardens in São Paulo. Situated on one of the city's main avenues, the roof-top pool of Unique Hotel stands out from its surroundings in form and in its choice of materials. The building into which this ruby is set is a post-modern masterpiece designed by the foremost Brazilian architect Ruy Ohtake in the shape of a gigantic folded table. Designer Gilberto Elkis's challenge was to respond effectively to this new city landmark.

On the ground-floor level, in front of the building's grand façade, Elkis framed the entrance by using tall, mature imperial palm trees planted in a row, which separate the busy avenue from the hotel. Between the palms and the building is a dry oasis, with islands composed of Portuguese mosaic, some arranged loosely, some compact. A long thread of water in a channel made of Cor-Ten steel winds through the site.

The strong design has an organically abstract but playful shape and was designed to be seen from above as well as from ground level. The snaking water element induces contemplation and evokes the question of where the water leads. To enhance the sculptural aspect of the design, the serpentine river is incorporated within mounds formed with loose mosaic tiling. The architectural plants *Pandanus utilis* and *Agave angustifolia* were introduced to intensify the otherworldly, desert-like scenery.

Near the building and next to the two main entrances are small islands edged with Cor-Ten steel and planted with large specimens of the sculptural *Beaucarnea recurvata*. On the corner of the street, several large Cor-Ten steel boxes, which will oxidize over time to a grey-brown or purple colour, were aligned and planted with the winter-flowering yellow *Tabebuia chrysotricha*.

On the roof terrace is the Skye restaurant, the presidential suite and the amazingly red swimming pool. Lined with brilliant red Vidrotil tiles, it suggests the opposites of hot and cold. 'I tried to play with the hot sensation that is provoked by the red colour that completely dissipates when people come into contact with the cold water,' says Elkis, 'and we created around it this enormous deck made from *ipê* wood, where we can sit and appreciate the beautiful São Paulo skyline.' The furniture for the terrace was carefully chosen to avoid competing with the view: chaise longues have a rectilinear design reminiscent of the timber boxes that seem to disappear into the decking. The boundary is made of glass to a height of 2.2 metres, forming a kind of wrap-around screen on which the whole city is projected.

In the evening, when the lights are down, thousands of bright lights from the neighbouring apartments can be seen from this roof garden, like miniature stars blending with those in the sky. It is simply a magical place to be.

below The key elements of Elkis's design are clearly laid out in the drawing: a line of palm trees separates the building from the busy avenue and the thin thread of water, designed to be seen from above as well as from ground level, snakes around the site.

opposite top left & centre Often used in conceptual or land art, Cor-Ten steel planters seem to have been dug from the soil, leaving voids lined with rocks, and placed randomly in the lawn.

opposite below & top right In a single gesture, the water channel traverses the garden, providing a cool lifeline in this arid, desert-like landscape.

trees & palms	shrubs & groundcover
Beaucarnea recurvata	Agave angustifolia
Pandanus utilis	Dracaena marginata
Tabebuia chrysotricha	Murraia paniculata
	Sanseviera trifasciata

Juxtaposing units of the same material – granite – but in different geometric shapes and sizes, Fiaschi created effective abstract patterns. Beyond, the plain green expanse of lawn opens up the garden.

06 spacious & elegant garden

luciano fiaschi | designer
location | são paolo

Now an exclusive residential area in São Paulo, in the early nineteenth century Morumbi was a huge sprawling farm belonging to an Englishman, John Rudge, completely given over to the cultivation of black tea. Later, parts of the farm were sold off in expensive plots to aristocratic members of society so that they could build their magnificent dream homes, far from the busy and noisy city centre. Today, the area is still much sought after, commanding some of the highest land prices in São Paulo. Leafy urban streets seem to retain a memory of the area's original vegetation and conceal secret gardens behind their genteel façades.

It is for one of these large old mansions that Luciano Fiaschi began work on this particular garden in 1987, simultaneously with the refurbishment of the interiors. A large bay-window seems to bring the natural world outside right into the house, and when Fiaschi was invited to design the garden one of his first concerns was how to exploit this opportunity to integrate interior and exterior spaces.

As in many Fiaschi projects, his answer to the challenge was to allow ample space for circulation and to open up views around the garden, rather than filling it with too many imposing and colourful plants. Lines that are long, precise and elegant define the major volumes, establishing the shape of the lawns and borders. Existing mature palm trees and pink *ipê* trees were retained, forming the upper storey of the planting, while Fiaschi worked on the middle and lower levels, stipulating shrubs and perennials. The client, a keen gardener, also requested a border to cultivate flowers all year round, and for this Fiaschi specified a combination of annuals and flowering plants that can be constantly replaced according to the seasons.

In the first phase Fiaschi worked primarily on the planting near the swimming pool, retaining the original paving around it. The tennis court was also preserved, and he concentrated more instead on landscaping the entrance to the garden and ensuring good access throughout. One of the distinctive features of this phase was an elegant retaining wall built in a great arc under the shade of the *ipe* trees, which can be used as seating all year round. Another is the bubbling fountain made of 'pedra sabão' soapstone.

Seven years later, Fiaschi was called on again to continue the landscape project. The tennis court was no longer in constant use and was replaced by a free and open lawn area in a sweeping curve. Turf steps, with borders for flowers, created a link to the new level.

In this second phase the highlight is the sloping area towards the games room where a rustic greenhouse was built to cultivate orchids – another passion of the owner. A brightly coloured array of exotic blooms thrives under the rustic timber slats. Fiaschi also suggested the installation of a tank to water them in dry weather. There, the clients can forget the stresses of the outside world while cultivating gorgeous orchid species; or they can entertain friends in a garden that, although unquestionably in an urban setting, seems to have space in abundance.

trees & palms

Chrysalidocarpus lutescens

Clusia minor

Euterpe edulis

Lagerstroemia indica

Phoenix roebelenii

Pinanga kuhlii

Tabebuia chrysotricha

shrubs & bamboos

Abelia grandiflora

Arundina bambusifolia

Bambusa gracilis

Calathea zebrina

Camellia japonica

Dichorisandra
  thyrsiflora

Gardenia jasminoides

Leea rubra

Ligustrum sinense

Nandina domestica

Rhododendron simsii

groundcover

Agapanthus africanus

Ajuga reptans

Alpinia purpurata

Anthurium andreanum

Aspidistra elatior

Asparagus densiflorus
  (Sprengeri)

Begonia coccinea

Chlorophytum comosum

Clivia miniata

Ctenanthe oppenheimiana
  tricolor

Cyclanthus bipartitus

Duranta repens

Evolvulus glomeratus

Fragaria australis

Heliconia brasiliensis

Heliconia latisphata

Heliconia rostrata

Impatiens walleriana

Iris germanica

Lantana camara

Neomarica caerulea

Ophiopogon japonicus

Russelia equisetiformis

Schizocentron elegans

Sellaginella sp.

Spathiphyllum cannifolium

Spathiphyllum wallisii

Vinca major 'Variegata'

Zebrina purpusii

Zoysia japonica

climbers & epiphytes

Abutilon megapotamicum

Hedera helix

Monstera deliciosa

Platycerium bifurcatum

Plumbago capensis

Strongylodon macrobotrys

In a rustic greenhouse, several species of exotic orchids thrive under the light shade provided by the timber slats. This small, enclosed structure contrasts with the large open spaces of lawn that Fiaschi incorporated in his plan for the garden.

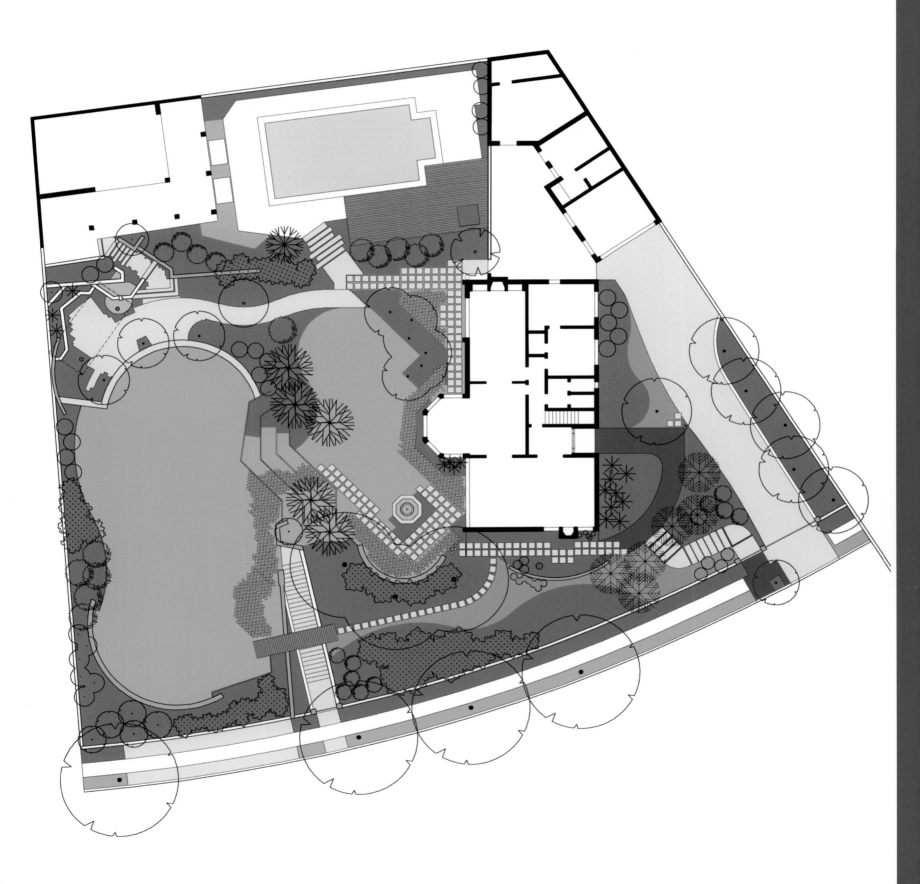

right Close to the house a border was created for the clients to cultivate seasonal plants, introducing a sense of change into the garden.

below In Luciano Fiaschi's designs, space is considered one of the most important aspects of the garden. From this angle, the generous sweep of lawn beyond the trees and broad steps gives the impression of an open expanse, even in this crowded urban context.

above left & right For the hard surfaces Fiaschi suggested Miracema stone in different formats and sizes, punctuated with areas of lawn. The same paving surrounds the bubbling fountain carved out of soapstone.

left The generous steps also use rustic Miracema granite, edged with thin strips of stone. Around the the lawn, the raised wall in a great arc can be used as a bench throughout the year.

sculpture

sculpture

Sculpture in the traditional sense is, by definition, something with built-in values of permanence, 'forever beautiful', something of a shape and material that 'defies time'. But then there is the other reality of the evanescent new – that truth born of the moment. Cherry blossoms in old Japan, or one jump ahead of obsolescence in the modern. I have thought of this, too, as sculpture.

Isamu Noguchi

In the same way that artists through the ages have carved models in stone and bone, or moulded them in clay or wax before casting them in bronze, so gardens demand an ongoing process of working and re-working in three-dimensional and visual interactions with the site. For gardens and gardeners, however, the fourth dimension – time – has also to be considered. And in addition to the traditional media of earth, wood and stone, landscape architects and garden designers also have available materials such as vegetation, water, fire, plastic and steel, to create new and exciting sculptural spaces.

As the world we live in becomes increasingly complex, fast and technologically driven, the human mind comes to expect a more sophisticated way of communicating ideas, whether we are using a mobile phone in the street, surfing the internet, watching an advertisement in the cinema or, in this case, sitting in a created outdoor space. The prosaic attitude of regarding a garden as a place simply to raise plants and create beauty has changed. Roberto Burle Marx, Luis Barragán, Isamu Noguchi, Kathryn Gustafson, Charles Jencks and many others have been instrumental in moving landscape design forwards and raising the subject to high art – a garden is now not merely a collection of plants but an art form in its own right. No longer does a garden represent only aesthetic ideals: it can also be a device to provoke us and make us re-evaluate our position in relation to the elements and each other. In the twentieth century gardens were reinvented as an outward manifestation of our unconscious thoughts about nature, and have now evolved to become Theatre.

In a literal sense, when the lines in a garden become three-dimensional we have the genesis of a potential sculptural space, but what makes true sculpture of a garden is the poetry hidden beneath, or embedded in, the communication between different forms in one, two and three dimensions.

In this chapter, sculptural forms appear in one guise in a garden by Anna Luiza Rothier, where natural boulders rise from a water feature to support a pergola. Gilberto Elkis plays with perspective and perception in his high-tech garden for a shop in São Paulo. We can explore a landscape where the concept of dunes inspired Lucia Porto on a grand scale and also admire the stunning minimalism of a garden by Marcelo Faisal.

Stone, wood and plants are the materials used by Maria Cecilia Gorski to create the Conjunto Nacional garden; while cool transparent glass forms the walls of a house and palms fronds appear to be the ceiling in Brunete Fraccaroli's exciting creation. Art and landscape merge in a grand design by Luciano Fiaschi, while the garden becomes sculpture in an austere and geometrical space designed by Alex Hanazaki.

previous pages A High-Tech Garden (p. 153).

opposite Japanese influence is evident in this design for a restaurant in São Paulo by Alex Hanazaki. Timber edging, gravel and clipped box form the lower level, while the upper level is filled with the sinuous stems and airy foliage of bamboos, set against dark wooden panels.

above left In this striking courtyard, Alex Hanazaki used a combination of materials to create a contemplative space with a minimal feel. The deck walkway, linking different parts of the building, is laid across a reflecting water feature. In the centre a line of small, round *Buxus sempervirens* guides the eye towards the *Pandanus* planted against a stone wall. Water flows gently down this daring, eight-metre-high wall to collect in the pool below.

above right Two of the major influences present in contemporary landscape design in Brazil combine in this neo-tropical-style garden by Marcelo Faisal: indigenous tropical flora and European garden and architectural sensibility inherited from the Colonial period. Oversized pots and frog add both sculptural forms and a touch of humour.

A column made of natural, rough boulders is both a structural and sculptural feature.

01 colour in the landscape

anna luiza rothier | designer
location | rio de janeiro

Dramatic colours and a strong sculptural use of stone are the revelations in this remote and spectacular house and garden built by the sea near Rio de Janeiro. In sympathy with the site, both the architect and the garden designer Anna Luiza Rothier incorporated materials and colours from the landscape – in the brilliant orange walls set against the dramatic blues of the sea, sky and pool, and the luxuriant dark green of the planted foliage. And everywhere there is ineluctable sense that you are far south, deep in the tropics.

House and garden were built on a steep slope on former agricultural land – the great-great-grandson of the original farm owners, still living there, divided the property into several generous plots. The clients, a young couple living the hectic 'carioca' lifestyle, bought one to fulfil their dream of creating a holiday and weekend retreat. In a successful integration of architecture and landscape design, the walk from the house down to the beach is completely free of obstructions such as walls or gates, and passes through mounds created by completely reshaping the land.

Rothier's design is also notable for the way that it integrates sculptural forms and natural materials to match the exuberant vegetation. Rough, uncut boulders are piled up to form columns rising from a water feature to support the wooden beams of a pergola, and rustic paving made of Brazilian São Tomé stone is laid randomly in gravel. 'It is a spontaneous garden,' says Rothier, 'very loose in shapes and textures, spreading the green against the deep blue sea.'

A smooth, reflecting water feature surrounds much of the house, and at the main entrance a continuation of the patio forms a bridge connecting garden and house. A simple, restrained composition of a single stone and several species of aquatic plants enhances the beauty of the setting, rather than competing with it.

Plants were selected that could not only cope with the less than ideal conditions of the garden's arid soil and exposure to the sea, but would positively thrive on them. Another requirement was ease of transplanting, so that coconut and palm trees could be brought in at a mature size, immediately giving the impression of having been there forever. As the property is used mainly for weekends and holidays, one priority was that the garden should be simple to maintain, with perennial plants that can withstand all types of weather and seasons. To disguise some of the less attractive and more functional parts of the building, Rothier used plants such as heliconias, *Chrysalidocarpus lutescens* and *Leea coccinea*, and climbers such as jasmine and allamanda.

A rock garden contains numerous different types of cactus and epiphytic plants – mainly bromeliads – which revel in the environment and create a spectacular display. In a more humid part of the garden, the large leaves of spathiphyllum and swaying grasses form a complimentary composition of foliage shape and texture; across the waterfront, groups of beautiful spiked agaves bask under the open sunny sky. Every feature and every single species, is, as Rothier says, 'in the right place'.

below At the main entrance to the house, the patio paved with São Tomé stone extends to form a bridge across the water feature, connecting house and garden.

opposite Natural materials – wood, stone, water and vegetation – and dramatic colours which dazzle in the strong sunlight, combine to create a garden that seems to have grown spontaneously from the landscape.

trees & palms	Heliconia psittacorum
Chrysalidocarpus lutescens	Spathiphyllum cannifolium
Delonix regia	**climbers**
shrubs	Allamanda cathartica
Agave angustifolia	Jasminum sp.
Leea coccinea	Philodendron sp.
groundcover	**aquatics**
Bromeliads	Cyperus papyrus
Festuca glauca	Nymphaea sp.

In a fully three-dimensional design, Gilberto Elkis integrated triangular Cor-Ten steel planters, suspended in the air from steel cables, and a dynamic, playful water feature.

02 a high-tech garden

gilberto elkis | designer
location | são paolo

No landscape designer can translate the spirit of the city of São Paulo into gardens better than Gilberto Elkis. In what is the most high-tech and avant-garde city in the country, his work follows the prevailing ideology, creating spaces that are always dramatic and dynamic, pushing the boundaries between art and landscape.

In one of the most commercial and fashionable areas in São Paulo, Elkis designed this garden for the 'HouseGarden' shop. An unpromising plot, the space was a confined area to the rear of the building, surrounded by high walls. Potentially claustrophobic, an element of transparency was provided by the façade made entirely of glass, leading the eye unimpeded from interior to exterior.

The formidable challenge consisted of creating verticality in the restricted space available. Often in such situations designers incorporate over-sized pots or introduce a change of levels, but in his innovative design Elkis seems to use the sky itself. In a bold gesture, he suspended large pyramidal planters made of Cor-Ten steel from steel cables, which dominate the aerial aspect of the garden. And to create more drama, he repeated them along the main axis, emphasizing the impression of length – a play of spatial perception achieved with triumphant success.

Another enchanting element of this garden is undoubtedly the water feature. 'I had this idea of working with water to create a direct integration between the inside and outside space,' explains Elkis, 'to give some character and dynamism to the area, and I thought about the idea of water moving inside wheels and flowing freely from the wall and collecting in a reflecting water feature.' His vision becomes reality as the water emerges from the wall through transparent wheels and flows from the outdoor space into the interior into an elegant pool of darkly reflective water in a black-painted tank. For the evening a final detail was added: in a tray placed in the middle of the mirror pool jets of fire dart up from between stones, creating a mystical atmosphere.

A limited number of materials were used in the hardscaping, including Cor-Ten steel and small, pale beige pebbles, to avoid the crowded and sometimes over-designed feel found in many small gardens. The planting is likewise very restrained, with light forms of bamboo enhancing the feeling of transparency and height. Annuals such as white impatiens brighten the composition and frangipani, *Plumeria rubra,* was planted both for architectural interest and fragrance.

When designing any garden the key is to know at what point to stop adding plants, materials and features. In this particular project, Elkis managed to go to the extreme without compromising simplicity.

| Plumeria rubra | Phyllostachys pubescens | Dietes bicolor | Catharanthus roseus | Ophiopogon japonicus |

above Viewed from the interior of the shop across the dark water feature, the airy foliage of the bamboos against the light seems to bring in the sky itself as an integral part of the design.

above right Rivers of plants sweeping through gravel and irregular stepping stones have the strength of simplicity found in Japanese gardens.

opposite The bamboo *Phyllostachys pubescens* was used for its sculptural canes to link sky and ground. Planting at the lower level included *Dietes iridiodes* and the long-flowering white impatiens.

Graphic lines of pebbles edged with dark plastic and carefully positioned natural stones make for a minimal composition designed for contemplation.

03 dunes

lucia porto | designer
location | são paolo

The Flextronic is a new technological hub situated in a huge park of over 500,000 square metres in Sorocaba, near São Paulo. It contains a Research and Development (R&D) centre, along with other buildings, plus service areas, heliport, sport and leisure areas and access. In designing a landscape for this industrial park, Lucia Porto's first creative considerations were to respect the natural characteristics of the area – a forest reserve – and to make use of the local resources by building an artificial lake as a way of taking advantage of a natural spring. Both aims were incorporated into a confident design, establishing a clear identity for the park and its building installations.

A walk between two of the buildings was designed as a visual and theatrical experience, encapsulating within it the conceptual idea of moving through a series of enormous grassy dunes, sculpted from the land itself. As in nature, a feeling of enclosure and seclusion from the outside world gives way suddenly and unexpectedly to open views of the wild greenery of the surrounding forest.

A restrained palette of plants was all that was necessary to complement this landscape concept, with flowering hedges and native trees used for particular emphasis. On the other side of the grass dunes Porto created an alameda – a tree-lined promenade – for pedestrians and drivers. Mature palm trees were planted in straight lines or in groups, standing out against the structures, an idea that was repeated successfully to link buildings elsewhere in the park. And to effect a gentle transition between the developed site and the natural reserve beyond, she introduced areas planted with trees with attractive flowers or with large canopies to provide shade.

Individual smaller gardens were specifically designed for particular sections, for instance the foyer and reception area, and there is also a much-loved – and prize-winning – interior garden in the production area. Designed for contemplation during long working days, staff can sit here and free their thoughts. Maintaining the motif of dunes, Porto used a surface of sand with graphic snaking lines of black cobbles retained by dark plastic edging. Sparsely planted bamboos with golden canes, as sinuous as the lines on the ground, glow in the sunlight. A few sculptural stones were carefully sited, as in a Japanese Zen garden. Water cascades like a transparent curtain down the glass façade, blurring the landscape beyond.

Numerous indoor gardens use the same language: cobbles and pebbles for the surface, stylized curving lines and low shrubs contrasting with three-dimensional bamboo. In a water feature around Building 01, large concrete rings containing aquatic plants defy logic by appearing to float.

Wandering around this landscape project is like walking through a work of art, where sculpture meets drawing, colour enhances volumes, lines are translated into edging and texture into paving. Unlike many other forms of art that can merely be looked at, however, the Flextronic industrial park can be experienced with all the senses.

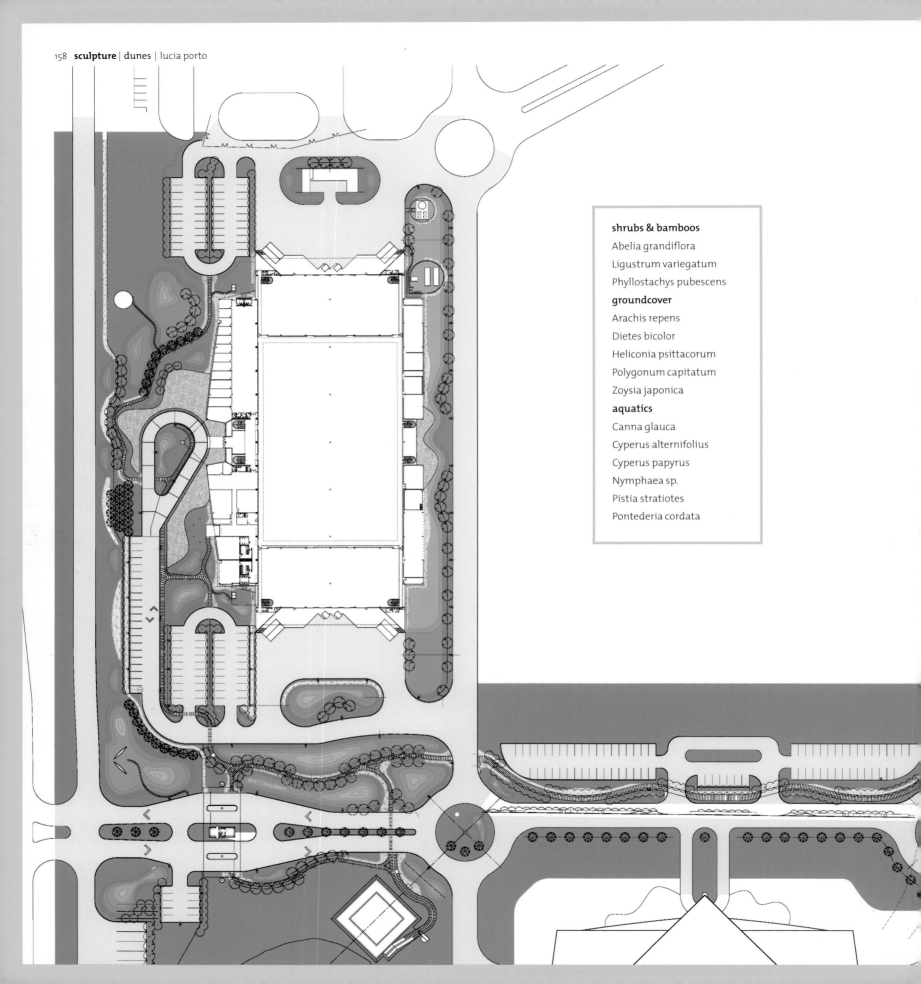

shrubs & bamboos
Abelia grandiflora
Ligustrum variegatum
Phyllostachys pubescens
groundcover
Arachis repens
Dietes bicolor
Heliconia psittacorum
Polygonum capitatum
Zoysia japonica
aquatics
Canna glauca
Cyperus alternifolius
Cyperus papyrus
Nymphaea sp.
Pistia stratiotes
Pontederia cordata

below, left & right A water feature almost
completely surrounds the glass and concrete
architecture. Specially selected rocks, large concrete
rings and aquatic plants break the uniformity of
the surface. Fountains add interest and the sprays
of mist create favourable conditions for the plants.
bottom In a gesture of respect to nature, Porto
retained the existing trees, irregularly spaced, in
the walkway leading to one of the buildings.

above left Concrete rings with aquatic plants appear to float inside the water feature – pebbles cover the surface to keep the soil in place.

above right A rational arrangement of concrete walls, gravel and planting – in this case *Buxus sempervirens*, *Dietes iridioides* and the bamboo *Phyllostachys pubescens* – is found even in this small corner of the grand project.

opposite The gigantic grass dunes create sculptural landmarks against the distant skyline. Flowering hedges provide colour while the seemingly impossibly tall, thin trees soar upwards, their canopies seeming to hover in the air.

A strongly axial orientation runs through Faisal's design for the garden – in this patio area architecture, hardscaping, decking, lawn and a line of *Myrciaria cauliflora* trees follow a strict alignment.

04 du plessis residence

marcelo faisal | designer
location | parati

A Luis Barragán inspired pure and minimalist house designed by Marcio Kogan and set in the Atlantic forest was the starting point for this landscape by Marcelo Faisal in Parati, near Rio de Janeiro. With Mies van der Rohe's dictum 'less is more' as inspiration, Faisal incorporates the modern and wilderness into one seamless space, in a remarkable project that respects plant individuality within an apparently unconscious design of rhythm, regularity and beauty.

To create impact at the entrance of the house he planted a single specimen of the Flamboyant tree, *Delonix regia*. This magnificent tree, with its red flowers in summer, contrasts well with the natural tones of the Mineira stone used in the building. The Flamboyant, with its spreading canopy and feathery leaves, has a maternal and embracing aspect, giving a strong emotional quality to the project. Along wall bases and beneath sculptural openings Faisal planted the iris-like flowering perennial *Dietes bicolor*.

To assimilate the wild tropical flora outside with the house's uncompromising modernism, Faisal created a clear, strong axis that runs along the façade of the house to the boundary of the property. In the space contained, called the 'Jabuticabeira patio', he strategically placed a line of *Myrciaria cauliflora* trees to create a visual perspective running from the entrance. This device can also be appreciated from within the building, where the trees follow another trajectory, leading from each bedroom of the house, making them the dominant visual element in the composition.

Following the line of the wooden decking which dictates the direction of circulation, Faisal planted *Thunbergia erecta*, a shrub native to tropical Africa and useful for hedging, with its abundant foliage and purple flowers. For the ground surface he used *Zoysia* grass as an emerald green carpet, making a refreshing contrast with the white mosaic of the patio. A transparent row of the coconut palm *Cocos nucifera* is planted parallel with the swimming pool, forming another link between the unruly Atlantic forest and the contained architectural structure of the house and garden.

With its streamlined simplicity and strict linearity, the uniqueness of the space amazes everyone who sees it. Faisal's light touch has ensured that the stark minimalism of the building, interior spaces, outdoor architecture, vegetation, swimming pool and Atlantic forest come together to create a beautiful, calm and otherworldly space.

left Minimalist architecture and stark white materials have a strong visual impact against the free-form background vegetation. The rectangular void in the wall is underplanted with *Dietes bicolor* and in the centre of the patio a single *Delonix regia* (Flamboyant) casts delicate shadows.

opposite The even placement of the specimens of ornamental *Myrciaria cauliflora* trees – almost like living columns – enhances the architectural feel of the patio area.

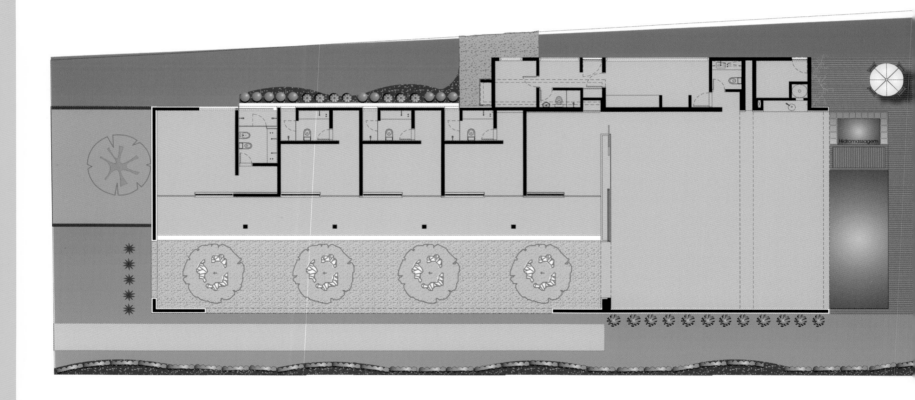

trees & palms	shrubs	groundcover	
Cocos nucifera	Thunbergia erecta	Dietes bicolor	Strelitzia augusta
Delonix regia	Viburnum tinus	Neomarica caerulea	Zoysia
Myrciaria cauliflora		Ophiopogon japonicus	
Podocarpus macrophyllus		'Nana'	

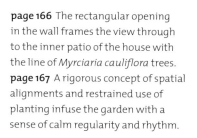

page 166 The rectangular opening in the wall frames the view through to the inner patio of the house with the line of *Myrciaria cauliflora* trees.
page 167 A rigorous concept of spatial alignments and restrained use of planting infuse the garden with a sense of calm regularity and rhythm.

far left Specially commissioned sculptures by Lígia Reinach sit well with the futuristic shapes of the architecture, glimpsed through the different plant textures.
left Paving is edged with red sandstone, used also to create the raised planting beds.
below A sinuous seat of *ipê* wood serves as a barrier separating the open access pedestrian zone from private areas, with *Chrysalidocarpus lutescens* forming a screen.

05 conjunto nacional

cecilia gorski | designer
location | são paolo

Regarded by the busy Paulista citizens as one of its major landmarks, the Conjunto Nacional building lies in the heart of the city. In the 1960s, its famous Fasano restaurant and delicatessen were the venue for glamorous, high-society parties. The building then suffered a period of decline until 1994, when a programme of renovation was initiated, which, it was hoped, would provide an inspirational example of urban regeneration for the entire Paulista Avenue. Following the refurbishment of the façade, pavement, gallery and other architectural features, landscape architect Cecilia Gorski was invited to integrate the building into its urban surroundings by creating a modernist garden.

At its heart is a spectacular round building looking like a flying saucer that has landed among the high-rise skyscrapers. Three other buildings delimit a terrace, with an enormous gallery on stilts on the ground floor and commercial offices above. The layout of the project evolved around this architectural grouping of structures and spaces.

One of Cecilia Gorsky's trademarks in this project was the use of stone. 'I like the way eastern civilizations use stones,' she says, 'and how they place them in the landscape'. For this project she used Brazilian rocks with different textures and contrasting colours – Miracema in various tones and red sandstone, punctuated sporadically with square blue tiles.

To control drainage on the terrace she used sculptural pots made of amianthus – a combination of asbestos and cement. Larger raised planters were clad with red stone set in thin horizontal strips in a style known as *canjiquinha*. Since the terrace is in effect a roof garden and cannot support a great weight of soil, some areas were covered instead with small rough grey stones that contrast well with the precisely cut Miracema stone and red sandstone edging. Forming a boundary between public pedestrian spaces and private areas belonging to the offices, and between the different textures of stone, is a bench made of *ipê* wood which snakes its way around the site.

Weight limitations also meant that the vegetation had to be placed strategically. Gorsky used large expanses of the bromeliad *Vriesea bituminosa*, mixed with large cobbles, while in circular planters fitted into the curves of the *ipê*-wood bench she planted the palm *Chrysalidocarpus lutescens* to screen the view of neighbouring buildings, as well as to create shade. And in the raised red sandstone beds are dramatic blocks of variegated *Ananas bracteatus*, whose red stripes and flowers are perfectly in harmony with the colours of the stone. Other species such as *Allamanda violacea*, *Clusia fluminensis* and tough *Phormium tenax* were used for their wind-resistant foliage and also because they are undemanding about soil and adaptable to varying amounts of sunlight.

For both old and new generations, the Conjunto Nacional is now a precious urban garden and an important part of Paulista Avenue tradition, serving as both a space to enjoy being in and a viewpoint for looking out at – and escaping from – the city.

trees & palms

Chrysalidocarpus lutescens

Clusia fluminensis

Phoenix roebelenii

shrubs

Agave americana

Jasminum mesnyi

Leea coccinea

Phormium tenax

Rhododendron sp.

Thunbergia erecta

groundcover

Ananas bracteatus

Chlorophytum comosum
 'Variegata'

Coleus verschafeltii

Kalanchoe tubiflora

Porphyrocoma lanceolata

Russelia equisetiformis

Schizocentron elegans

Vriesea bituminosa

Zantedeschia aethiopica

climbers

Allamanda violacea

Hedera canariensis

Philodendron erubescens 'Gold'

Philodendron sellowii

Plumbago capensis

Syngonium podophyllum

aquatics

Cyperus papyrus

Spathiphyllum 'Mauna Loa'

Typhonodorum lindleyanum

opposite above The multiple stems of the palm *Chrysalidocarpus lutescens* create fantastic shadow-plays on the tall white wall and the paving below.

opposite below A perforated brick wall filters light and wind and provides a strong backdrop for the *Phoenix roebelenii* planted in containers. The curving *ipê* wood bench winds its way around the site in a seemingly infinite journey

left In this overwhelmingly urban setting skyscrapers on Paulista Avenue tower over the garden – a green oasis for Paulistas. Raised beds built *canjiquinha*-style with red arenito stone are planted with *Clusia fluminensis*, *Ananas bracteatus* and *Agave americana*.

opposite A limited range of materials and plants were chosen that were tough, durable and easy to maintain, as well as creating rhythm and cohesion. Exuberant architectural plants inject vibrancy, anchored by a formal backbone.

The play of light, reflection, transparency and exotic plants make this glass box greater than the sum of its parts. In this surreal world, house becomes garden and garden becomes house – the trunks and fronds of palm trees form part of the architecture.

06 inside out

brunete fraccaroli | designer

location | são paolo

Every year a major garden and house show takes place in the main cities of Brazil. Celebrating the eve of the new millennium in 1999 in São Paulo, interior designer Brunete Fraccaroli created Deca Space, a sculptural glass box built in the middle of a garden. The transparency of the material challenges the concept of the outside garden, with nature presented in every angle, even on the walls and ceiling of the rooms.

Between the house and the monumental glass box, within a 200-square-metre area, Fraccaroli, in collaboration with garden designer Gilberto Elkis, planted balls of box, *Buxus sempervirens*, in a formal composition, with trees in the middle of the beds to add height. Next to the transparent room a square box hedge is used as an elegant accent against the glass.

Inside the glass room are imperial palm trees, with their long trunks breaking out of the glass roof to create a natural canopy as ceiling decoration. Despite the encroaching nature, the feeling inside the transparent space is cool and contemporary – modern sofas, a high-tech television set, designer chairs by the renowned Campana brothers, a high-end kitchen, even an acrylic box for the bathroom. To complement the inside-out concept white orchids are used in planters, with a stainless-steel water feature as a focal point.

The choice of materials could not be grander: white carrara marble laid inside and outside the glass box is supported by a Cor-Ten steel edge. The steel and glass columns bind all the elements together in this surreal ensemble. As a reflective cube and bright tunnel in the middle of the garden, Fraccaroli's design points to a new era of garden design. Her sleek, highly modern space exists in complete harmony with the tropical Brazilian flora, redefining the concept of an indoor-outdoor room while integrating it seamlessly into nature.

above left & right White, used for units in the bathroom area and for furniture, ensures that the effect of the surrounding green is maximized.
opposite Reflections and refractions of the gigantic leaves of the palms and other exotic trees decorate the transparent walls of this sculptural glass box. White orchids bring their cool poise to a sleek modern design.

palms
Roystonea regia
shrubs
Buxus sempervirens
Myrtus communis
Viburnum tinus
aquatics
Cyperus papyrus
Cyperus alternifolius

opposite above Red stone, pink mosaic, rough granite and compacted cobbles contribute different colours and textures to the water feature.
opposite below Garden design and landscape art merge in the circular patio, cut through by the path that sweeps around the entire garden.

07 landscape as art

luciano fiaschi | designer
location | itatiba

The Quinta da Baroneza district of Itatiba, north of São Paulo, is a high standard development, with golf course, lakes and an extensive area of preserved native forest. The clients for this project initially bought two standard double-sized plots of 3,000 square metres, making the whole property more than half a hectare (about 1.5 acres), and, to develop their garden further, they recently extended it again.

Architect Marco Passarelli visualized the residence as two blocks covered by flat roofs, linked by a third with a terracotta roof, opening out on to a long rectangular swimming pool. In response, designer Luciano Fiaschi performed an amazing transformation of the surrounding site into a work of landscape art. Groundbreaking, professional and from an older generation of landscape architects, Fiaschi draws inspiration from many sources, but the strong influence of Eckbo and the American modernist movement is evident in his use of open spaces, long lines and intricate shapes. But in Fiaschi's work lines are not merely lines; they seem to belong to another sphere, where they become poetry.

From the house a lawn extends almost uninterrupted to the edges of the property. 'The client asked for this ample space, hence in this garden there are no hedges or other visual obstructions,' says Fiaschi. Instead, the brief was for a site to display the client's sculptures, most of them by renowned Brazilian artists such as Franz Weissmann, Emanoel Araújo and Adriana Banfi.

Fiaschi specified red arenito sandstone for the entrance steps to the swimming pool and the sculptural wall, of varying heights, which surrounds the space. From outside, the contrast between the red, natural stone and the white, modern architecture is arresting. Modulations in tone from red to pink, such as clear red Portuguese mosaic on the path and rustic pinkish granite for the patio, are subtly repeated throughout.

An original and distinctive water feature is carefully sited near the house, cleverly linked to the swimming pool and flowing under thin strips of stone. Large natural cobbles were used as a surface, compacted so that the clients and friends could walk barefoot on them and play in the water.

Vegetation is simple and monochromatic, following the clients' request that all flowers should be white to echo the white of the architecture. The only exceptions are the small yellow flowers of the *Caesalpinia ferrea* trees in the car park. From here, a virtuoso arrangement of steps leads to two paths. The first follows an arc to the house and swimming pool. The second, made of 'desempenado' concrete takes a great sweep around the entire property. Along the way trees are planted in a groups – still young, they promise a future of magnificent spreading canopies.

A sense of destination is crucial in a garden – a hidden secret waiting to be discovered or just a place to rest. Fiaschi realized this with style in a patio made of concentric circles of pink granite sets, with irregular gaps and edges blurred with grass, and curved, rough-cut, stone seats. In the middle is a bonfire for evenings, creating another ethereal and mystical element in this work of landscape art.

trees & palms
Archontophoenix cunninghamii
Beaucarnea recurvata
Bismarckia nobilis
Caesalpinia ferrea
Citrus sp.
Clusia minor
Cocos nucifera
Eugenia sp.
Magnolia x soulangeana
Myrciaria cauliflora
Pandanus utilis

Plumeria alba
Socratea exorrhiza
Swartzia langsdorfii
Tabebuia sp.
shrubs & bamboos
Bambusa gracilis
Bauhinea variegata
 'Candida'
Cordia leucocephala
Cordia superba
Gardenia sp.
Phyllostachys pubescens

Punica granatum
Rhododendron simsii
groundcover
Agapanthus africanus
Chlorophytum comosum
Dietes grandiflora
Eragrostis curvula
Evolvulus pusillus
Lycianthes asarifolia
Ophiopogon japonicus
Pandanus racemosus
Pennisetum setaceum

Russelia equisetiformis
Stenotaphrum secundatum
Strelitzia augusta
Vriesea imperialis
climbers
Philodendron martianum
Plumbago capensis

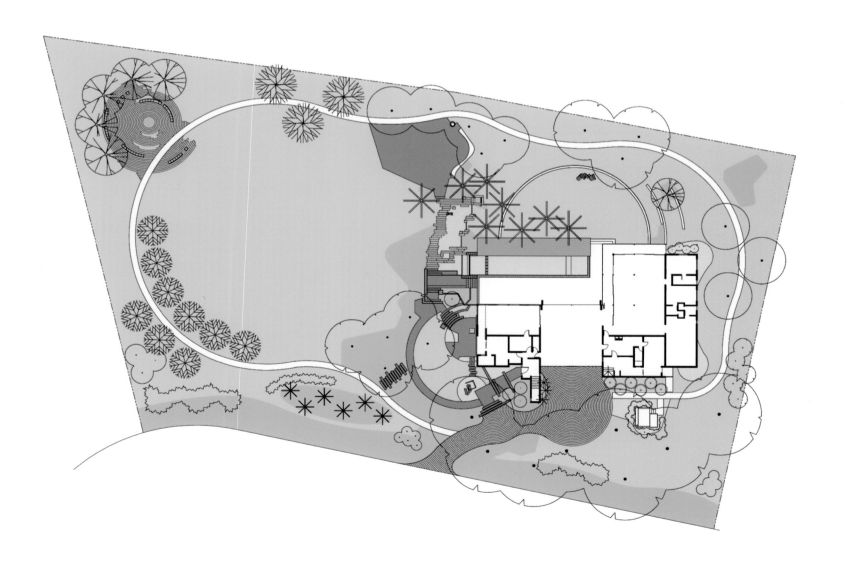

above left Complimentary tones of red stone and green vegetation contrast well with the white, modernist architecture.

above, centre & right, & below In Luciano Fiaschi's universe, steps are not only designed as a mundane mechanical device for getting from one level to another, they are sculpture in their own right. They also provide a monumental and sympathetic platform for works of art. Wide expanses of space kept deliberately free from visual obstructions make the garden a perfect setting for the client's important collection of sculpture.

above Low retaining walls in both continuous and broken arcs conform to the concentric shape of the overall concept of the garden. They also serve a practical function as they were designed to hold back soil on slopes and to provide seating.

above Open spaces, long sweeping lines and intricate, intersecting shapes are hallmarks of Fiaschi's work. A continuous path around the entire property takes people on a journey through the various elements of the landscape .

The austere, geometrical planting design is composed mainly of pruned viburnum, hedges of *Buxus sempervirens* and the architectural Phoenix palm.

08 sculptural formality

alex hanazaki | designer
location | são paolo

Located in a privileged area in São Paulo, this historically significant Colonial-style residence was built in 1904 as the Francisco Matarazzo hospital and is now a protected building listed by the Brazilian heritage agency (Condephaat). In the space around three sides of the building that had once been a car park, landscape architect Alex Hanazaki created this magnificent garden. In Hanazaki's view the garden works as a large outdoor room, with the trees surrounding the building providing a natural ceiling with their large, spreading canopies.

Formal inspiration and references came from the elegant historic squares of the city. Sculptural trees and vegetation left in their natural, untamed forms contrast with geometrically clipped and arranged topiary. The intention of the designer is clearly visible in his playful use of the geometry of the viburnums pruned to match exactly the shape and size of the timber seats, and in the enormous *Phoenix* palms soaring above, performing a silent ballet in air. 'I like to provoke and create sensations. The garden has to have interactivity with the people who are going to use it,' explains Hanazaki. 'I never try to find inspiration in anything ready-made. My inspiration is nature, and I try to understand why it is the way it is.'

Unfolding dramatically along a long central walkway that encircles the building, the garden conceals warm and intimate spaces for contemplation. At one end is a restful water feature and a wider space for relaxation. For the central axis the designer selected white ceramic tiles; between large sections thus formed he placed strips of lighting that produce a colourful visual effect, emphasizing the garden's perspective. From one extreme of the garden to the other, visitors experience an endless green labyrinth that recalls French gardens – interpreted with a twist into an exciting new language.

The grandson of Japanese immigrants, Hanazaki is proud of his cultural inheritance and ancestry. 'I have never created an Oriental garden, but most of my work has something of the Oriental culture.' Hanazaki's Japanese background is evident in the geometrical austerity of the planting design: there is architectural symmetry in the regularly spaced *Myrciaria* trees, all more than a hundred years old and looking as if they had been there a lifetime. The sword-shaped leaves of the *Pandanus* create drama, while the foliage of the palm trees add lightness and movement.

Sculptures placed in the garden engage with the space, as sculptures always have in Hanazaki's work. Adriana Riskallah created an installation for evenings. Entitled *Moons*, a series of white globes installed on the trunk of the *Caesalpinia peltophoroides* glow above the uplighters and sway gently in the wind. The furniture was carefully selected and placed with the public in mind so as to provide comfort and offer perspectives from which to appreciate the garden and its artworks.

trees	Pandanus utilis	Cycas circinalis
Caesalpinia peltophoroides	Phoenix roebelenii	Ligustrum sinensis
Ficus benjamina	**shrubs**	Rhododendron simsii
Myrciaria cauliflora	Buxus sempervirens	Viburnum tinus

above Giant blue-glazed planters containing palms dwarf formal topiary blocks and guide the view down the length of the garden.

opposite A sculpture by Adriana Riskallah echoes the sculptural *Pandanus*.

top Lighting set into the ground accentuates the striking, almost otherworldly, fronds of the palm trees.

above *Moons*, a sculptural installation by Adriana Riskallah, glow in front of the stark forms of the uplit *Myrciaria* trees.

right The theatrical landscape of Alex Hanazaki takes on a different reality in the evening when the lighting produces a series of dramatic visual effects, transforming both natural and man-made features.

further reading

Adams, William Howard, *Roberto Burle Marx: The Unnatural Art of the Garden*.
    New York, Museum of Modern Art, 1991.
Arquitetos e Paisagistas (Yearbook). São Paulo, G & A Editorial.
Burle Marx, Roberto. *Arte e Paisagem* (*Art and Landscape*).
    São Paulo, Editorial Nobel, 1987.
Burle Marx, Roberto, Ono, Haruyoshi & Tabacow, José. *Plantas bem brasilieras
    presentadas por Burle Marx* (The Plants of Brazil Presented by Burle Marx).
    Rio de Janeiro, Rio Editora, 1980.
Dourado, Guilherme Mazza, *Visoes de Paisagem: um panorama do
    paisagismo contemporaneo no Brazil* (*Visions of Landscape:
    A Panorama of Contemporary Landscapes in Brazil*).
    Associacao Brasileira de Arquitetos Paisagistas, São Paulo, 1997.
Jardins do Brasil. São Paulo, G & A Editorial.
Leenhardt, Jacques, *Nos Jardins de Burle Marx*. São Paulo, Perspectiva, 1994.
Montero, Marta Iris, *Burle Marx. The Lyrical Landscape*.
    London, Thames & Hudson; Berkeley, University of California Press, 2000.
Natureza, edição especial, *Os mais belos jardins tropicais do brasil*.
    Editora Europa, 2000.
Soares, Silvio Macedo, *Quadro do Paisagismo no Brasil*
    (*Landscape Design in Brazil*). São Paulo, Gráfica Pancrom, 1999.
Vaccarino, Roassana (ed.), *Roberto Burle Marx: Landscapes Reflected*.
    New York, Princeton Architectural Press, 2000.
Warren, William, *Tropical Garden Plants*.
    London & New York, Thames & Hudson, 2005.
Waymark, Janet, *Modern Garden Design. Innovation since 1900*.
    London & New York, Thames & Hudson, 2003.
Wijaya, Made, *Tropical Garden Design*. London, Thames & Hudson, 2003.

magazines

Arbitare, Brazil.
Jornal da Paisagem
www.jornaldapaisagem.com.br
Leenhardt, Jacques, Utopian Renaissance. *Landscape Design*, 1996

sources of quotes

p. 6, 'The flora of...' William Howard Adams, *Nature Perfected. Gardens through
History*. New York, Abbeville, 1991.

p. 8 'Literature that authoritatively...', 'Letteratura della complessita', *Arbitare*,
Brazil.

p. 14 'The pool is...' Thomas D. Church, *Gardens are for People*. Berkeley, University
of California Press, paperback edition, 1995.

p. 62 'The value of the...' Roberto Burle Marx, *Arte e Paisagem*. São Paulo, Editorial
Nobel, 1987.

p. 114 'Of all arts...' Kandinsky, Wassily, *Concerning the Spiritual in Art*, 1912.

p. 146 'Sculpture in the traditional sense...' Torres, Ana Maria, *Isamu Noguchi: A
Study of Place*. New York, The Monacelli Press, 2000.

list of practices

Roberto Silva
    LandRob7@aol.com
    www.silvalandscapes.com

Ana Maria Bovério
    Trav. Álvares de Azevedo 110, Cambui
    Campinas, SP 13025–030
    tel (19) 3253 1004
    Anamboverio@terra.com.br

Orlando Busarello
    Av. Candido de Abreu, 526–15°, cj 1510A
    Curitiba, PR 80530–905
    tel/fax (41) 253 1334
    projetos@slompbusarello.com.br
    www.slompbusarello.com.br

Fernando Chacel
    Av. Almirante Barroso 22, sala 1406
    Rio de Janeiro, RJ 20031–000
    tel. (21) 2215 5307; 2215 5058; tel/fax 2215 1903
    fmchacel@novanet.com.br

Anna Maria Prado Dantas
    Rua Consolação 3396, apt. 144,
    Cerqueira César, São Paulo, SP 01416-000
    tel (11) 3083 0174
    anna.dantas@uol.com.br
    www.annadantaspaisagismo.com.br

Isabel Duprat
    Alameda Ministro Rocha Azevedo, 456, 5°, cj 92,
    São Paulo, SP 01410-000
    tel (11) 3088 1826 / fax (11) 3083 1728
    Isabelduprat@uol.com.br

Gilberto Elkis
Rua Rodésia 497, Vila Madelena,
São Paulo, SP 05435–020
tel/fax (11) 3815 9537
gilberto@elkispaisagismo.com.br

Marcelo Faisal
Av. São Gualter, 999, Alto de Pinheiros,
São Paulo, SP 05455–001
tel (11) 3021 2665, 3061 2674
projeto@marcelofaisal.com.br

Gil Fialho
R. João Moura, São Paulo, SP 05412–001
tel (11) 3062 4375; fax (11) 3018 9083
gilfialho@uol.com.br
www.gilfialho.com.br

Luciano Fiaschi
Rua Iperoig 910, São Paulo, SP 05016–000
tel (11) 3865 8034; fax 3862 3537
lfpaisagismo@uol.com.br

Brunete Fraccaroli
Rua Guarara, 261, apt. 71,
São Paulo, SP 01425–001
tel (11) 3885 8309; fax 3887 6834
brunete@osite.com.br

Evani Kuperman Franco
Rua Mourato Coelho, 798 – cj 52,
São Paulo, SP 05417 - 001
tel (11) 3812 5671
Evani@ekf.com.br
www.ekf.com.br

Cecilia Gorski
Rua Fernão Dias 186, São Paulo, SP 05427–000
tel/fax (11) 3034 1184
bgorski@terra.com.br

Alex Hanazaki
Rua Francisco Leitao 240
tel (11) 306 13420
alexhanazaki@uol.com.br

Sonia Infante
Estrada União e Indústria 11407
Itaipava, Petrópolis, RJ 25750–220
tel (24) 222-1172
arteiro@arteiro.com.br

Jamil Jose Kfouri
Alameda Rio Claro 95, apt. 162, Bela Vista,
São Paulo, SP 01332–010
tel/fax: (11) 3287 3711
jjk@sti.com.br

Eduardo Luppi
Rua Calógero Cália 501, cj.23,
Jardim da Saúde, São Paulo, SP 04152–101
tel (11) 5073.9422; fax. (11) 5594 6433
luppi@uol.com.br

Guilhermina Machado
R. Jose Americo de Goveia, 10, bl 01 casa 105,
Condominio Laguna Park,
Recreio dos Bandeirantes
Rio de Janeiro, RJ 22795–040
tel (21) 3150 9581; fax 3150 9580
guilhermina@guilhermina.com.br
www.guilhermina.com.br

Sergio Menon
Av Morumbi 1725,
São Paulo, SP 05607 –100
tel (11) 3814 4956; 3814 4931
Smenon@uol.com.br
www.gramaeflor.com.br

Elza Niero
Rua Bennet 67, São Paulo, SP 05464–010
tel/fax (11) 3021 6403
elzaniero@terra.com.br

Marcelo Novaes
Rua João de Castro Pupo Nogueira, 110
Campinas, SP 13094–520
tel (19) 3296 4455
paisagismo@marcelonovaes.com
www.marcelonovaes.com.br

Haruyoshi Ono
Rua Alice 29, Laranjeiras,
Rio de Janeiro, RJ 22241–020
tel (21) 2558 3048/2558 3235
fax (21) 2285 4669
escritorio@burlemarx.com.br

Luiz Carlos Orsini
Rua Engenheiro Teodoro Vaz 145
Luxemburgo, Belo Horizonte, MG 30380–330
fax (31) 3296 6455
yapo@pla.com.br

Maringa Pilz and Barbara Uccello
Rua Capitão Antonio Rosa 63, Jd. Paulistano
São Paulo, SP 01443 – 010
tel (11) 8256 9781; 3085 6560
mbjardins@uol.com.br

Lucia Porto
Av. Pedroso de Moraes 1853
Pinheiros, São Paulo, SP 05419–001
tel (11) 3812 3170; fax (11) 3819 2715
arquitetura@sidonioporto.com.br
www.sidonioporto.com.br

Anna Luiza Rothier
Av. Prefeito Mendes de Moraes 1250, apt. 501,
Rio de Janeiro, RJ 22610–090
tel (21) 3322 6893, 3322 6249; fax (21) 2422 0180
Annaluizarothier@uol.com.br

Iza Vieira Ruprecht
Rua Parapeti 15, Riviera Paulista
São Paulo, SP 04928–170
tel/fax (11) 5517 6139
ivsr@uol.com.br

Suely Suchodolsky
3610 Yacht Club Drive, Suite 604,
Aventura, Florida, FL 33180, USA
suelyland@aol.com.br
tel 3875 4545

Luiz Vieira
Av. Domingos Ferreira 4060 s 904
Boa Viagem, Recife, PE 51021-040
tel/fax (81) 3466 5812
lvarqp@elogica.com.br

acknowledgments

I would like to thank all the landscape and garden designers in Brazil for contributing their wonderful creations to this book: Marcelo Faisal, Gilberto Elkis, Lucia Porto, Eduardo Luppi, Luiz Vieira, Maringa Pilz, Barbara Uccello, Gil Fialho, Jamil Jose Kfouri, Sergio Menon, Evani Kuperman Franco, Guilhermina Machado, Iza Vieira Ruprecht, Orlando Busarello, Anna Maria Prado Dantas, Isabel Duprat, Sonia Infante, Luiz Carlos Orsini, Marcelo Novaes, Ana Maria Bovério, Suely Suchodolsky, Elza Niero, Luciano Fiaschi, Anna Luiza Rothier, Cecilia Gorski, Brunete Fraccaroli and Alex Hanazaki. Also *Natureza* magazine and Haruyosho Ono for supplying the Burle Marx photos for the introduction. A huge thanks to Roger N. Phillips and Victoria Cantwell for kindly helping me with the text. I also would like to thank Niki Medlik for designing this book as a work of art and the editorial staff at Thames & Hudson. A special thanks to Lucas Dietrich who supported this project from the beginning.

picture credits